Modernisation and Revolution

Bill Brugger and Kate Hannan

FLINDERS POLITICS MONOGRAPHS — No. 2

CROOM HELM
London & Canberra

©1983 B. Brugger, K. Hannan
Croom Helm Ltd, Provident House, Burrell Row,
Beckenham, Kent BR3 1AT

British Library Cataloguing in Publication Data
Brugger, Bill
     Modernisation and revolution.—(Flinders
     politics monographs; no. 2)
     1. Social change—political aspects
     I. Title   II. Hannan, Kate   III. Series
     303.4   HM101
     ISBN 0–7099–0695–1

Printed in Great Britain by
Biddles Ltd, Guildford, Surrey

TABLE OF CONTENTS

FLINDERS POLITICS MONOGRAPHS

A Series of Monographs in Politics and Related Disciplines

Series Editor: Dean Jaensch
Flinders University

The Flinders Politics Monographs consist of discrete studies of topics, themes and contemporary political issues which will be of interest to a wide audience in the Social Sciences.

The Series is edited in the Discipline of Politics, Flinders University, South Australia. Authors proposing a manuscript for inclusion in the Series should first send a brief abstract to:

The Editor,
Flinders Politics Monographs,
Discipline of Politics,
Flinders University,
Bedford Park,
South Australia, 5042.

TITLES ALREADY PUBLISHED IN THIS SERIES:

1. **N. Tracy**, *The Origins of the Social Democratic Party*

1.
MODERNISATION AND REVOLUTION IN EAST AND WEST

How did the 'modern' industrial societies of East and West get to be the way they are? Was revolution a necessary part of that development and what are the prospects for revolution today?

What, moreover, does it mean to be 'modern'? For many people the answer is self-evident. Modernisation consists in an improving standard of living based on rising productivity. Others add to this a set of behavioural characteristics in which social worth becomes seen in terms of achievement, 'instrumental rationality' and the like. More broadly modernisation may be seen in terms of a movement from 'community' with a very simple division of labour to 'association' with a very elaborate network of interrelated roles and structures. Still others cast modernisation in terms of the growth of law or more particularly of contract law as opposed to law which prescribes rights and duties according to status. Much of contemporary sociology consists in working out a taxonomy of what it means to be 'modern' and consigning everything else into the category of 'traditional'. What is overlooked is that a particular society (such as the United States of America) is often taken to epitomise modernisation and the necessary features of modernisation are no more than generalisations from that particularity. Such an approach we shall call <u>ethnocentric</u>. Other approaches which distinguish between different types of modernity epitomised by different societies (such as the Soviet Union or America) we shall call <u>multilinear</u>. Either category might be cast in terms of market relations, economic growth, patterns of behaviour or the achievement of particular kinds of political system.

A different way of defining progress (modernisation) is in terms of some historical 'essence'. The German philosopher Hegel saw the whole of history in terms of the development of the rational and universal Mind (<u>Zeitgeist</u>) towards self-consciousness and freedom. Progress, therefore, might be measured in terms of the attainment of freedom both from nature and from the arbitrary domination of one's fellows. As Hegel saw it, freedom might only be attained by participation in political life, and thus a developed state was one which allowed for an increasing pursuit of rationality and freedom. In the Hegelian tradition, the material world had historical significance only in terms of the unfolding of the rational Mind which was an objective entity in its own right, independent of the subjective minds of individual citizens.

By inverting Hegel, however, it is possible to see progress as the result of material determinants. The crudest materialist view portrays science and technology as though they possessed a logic of their own and were able to dictate to humankind the relationship between freedom and necessity. A more sophisticated materialist view, exemplified in the writings of Karl Marx, seeks to incorporate the technological and the human by casting history as the ceaseless resolution of contradictions between the 'productive forces' and the 'relations of production'.[1] In particular, the resolution of the contradiction between advanced productive forces and backward relations of production takes the form of a sequence of modes of production. But what gives rise to the contradiction in the first place? Two sorts of answers are usually given. Either one falls back to a form of technological determinism (in the manner of Josef Stalin)[2] or to a form of objective idealism (in the manner of Georgy Lukacs).[3] Theorists find it extremely difficult to explicate a dialectic which reconciles the two.

The term 'revolution' is as difficult to define as the term 'modernisation'. At the risk of oversimplification, we shall outline three ways by which a definition might be constructed. The first of these sees revolution as a fundamental change in the value system which informs a society. This <u>cultural</u> definition would include the notion of 'scientific revolution' which consists in what the philosopher Thomas Kuhn calls a 'paradigm shift' - a shift in the framework of concepts in which people look

---

1.   These productive forces (the way human beings confront and interact with nature to produce their means of subsistence) include the instruments of production, the raw materials, the organisation of human labour and its skills and the way these elements are combined (i.e. forms of co-operation and co-ordination). The relations of production consist, on the one hand, in the relationship of humans to the productive forces and, on the other, in their relationships with each other in social groups. These relations of production may be broken down into three elements - the ownership of the means of production, the technical division of labour and the reciprocal relationship between patterns of production and patterns of distribution of the social product.

2.   J. Stalin, 'Dialectical and Historical Materialism', September 1938, in J. Stalin, <u>Problems of Leninism,</u> Foreign Languages Publishing House, Moscow, 1947, pp. 569-95.

3.   G. Lukacs, <u>History and Class Consciousness: Studies in Marxist Dialectics,</u> Merlin Press, London, 1971. In his Introduction to this collection of essays Lukacs states that he has attempted to chart a course between his 'passion for revolutionary messianism' and his political activism that had called for pragmatic political decisions within the Hungarian Communist Party. And yet, the overwhelming view conveyed to the reader of this essay collection is one whereby history is destined to culminate in the proletarian class consciousness that will facilitate the proletariat becoming the identical subject - object of history. It is a view described as 'standing Hegel on his feet': a view Lukacs describes as 'the authentic realisation' of Hegel's <u>Phenomenology of the Mind</u>: a view that this essay refers to as 'objective idealism'.

2.

at the world.[4] The second approach, deriving from political economy (not necessarily Marxian), sees revolution as a change in the dominant mode of production and hence the nature of the ruling class. This <u>political economy</u> definition would cover such occurrences as the 'bourgeois revolution' where the capitalist mode of production came to dominate the feudal and Burnham's 'managerial revolution' where, it is claimed, the old bourgeoisie is everywhere ceding power to a new managerial class.[5] The third approach, perhaps the most common use of the term revolution, is simply the overthrow of a regime by collective violence. This <u>narrowly political</u> definition, by focussing on the overthrow of a regime, would exclude palace coups which overthrow particular governments but is not so broad as to encompass the overthrow of a social order.

We have suggested four ways of defining modernisation and three ways of defining revolution. These are summarised in the following table:

Modernisation	Revolution
Ethnocentric	Cultural
Multilinear	Political-economic
Objective idealist	Narrowly political
Technological determinist	

We must stress that these categories are not mutually exclusive; the various theorists considered in this chapter have used different definitions at different times. Marx, for example, uses the term revolution both in the political-economic sense and in the narrowly political sense. The sociologist Max Weber uses revolution both in the political-economic and cultural sense, asserting merely a coincidence between the two.[6] A later sociologist W.F. Wertheim confuses revolution in all three senses and hovers between the multilinear view of modernisation and the objective idealist one.[7] An already confusing picture is further complicated by the tendency for some theorists, following Edmund Burke, to see modernisation only within the context of a national tradition; such a position we will call <u>relativist</u>. This essay will attempt to bring some order to the confusion by exemplifying the four approaches to modernisation and exploring the implications for revolution.

---

4.   See T. Kuhn, <u>The Structure of Scientific Revolutions,</u> 2nd enlarged edn., University of Chicago Press, Chicago, 1970. A view of political revolutions as characterised by similar value shifts is P. Schrecker, 'Revolution as a Problem in the Philosophy of History', <u>Nomus VIII: Revolution,</u> New York, 1967, pp 34-52.

5.   J. Burnham, <u>The Managerial Revolution</u> (1941), Penguin, Harmondsworth, 1945.

6.   M. Weber, <u>The Protestant Ethic and the Spirit of Capitalism,</u> Allen and Unwin, London, 1978.

7.   W. Wertheim, <u>Evolution and Revolution: The Rising Waves of Emancipation,</u> Penguin, Harmondsworth, 1974.

The Ethnocentric View

Social thought in all societies at most times in their history has been ethnocentric if not downright chauvinist. The world has been divided into the 'civilised' and the 'barbarians' and it was never too clear which would triumph.

The Roman Empire did quite well for a time by granting Roman citizenship to 'barbarians' and by convincing local rulers (by persuasion and conquest) that economic prosperity depended upon the institutions which upheld Roman law. The word 'progress' existed, but in its verbal form it was what armies did and as an abstract noun applied to history it was no more than the march of events. Yet there was a sense in which marginal societies were seen to be developing towards the pax Romana. There was no notion of social revolution (even though the origin of that word also was Latin) and even the Greek view, of a revolving sequence of forms of government (monarchy/tyranny, aristocracy/oligarchy, polyarchy/democracy) had paled before a system which seemed there to stay. Revolution, in Aristotle's sense of stasis, there indeed was, and the central government in Rome was overthrown several times - but after the advent of Augustus the regime did not change for several hundred years.

If there was an implicit notion of development in ancient Rome, it had no place for revolution - except perhaps the one which had brought the Augustan state into being. At the other end of the world, the Han Empire was legitimised by a similar set of beliefs. But the collapse of the Roman Empire and the Han dynasty in China revived in the West the notion of revolution as the Greek cycle of birth, death and rebirth and in China the similar notion of a dynastic cycle. The 'dark ages' in the West were defined as such in terms not only of Christian but also of Roman values and 'barbarian' empires sought legitimacy in Roman symbols. Similarly, in China, the repeated 'barbarian' conquests of the next millenium-and-a-half resulted in the establishment of agrarian bureaucracies modelled on the Han dynasty and legitimised by Han Confucian values. In both East and West there was much cultural diffusion. Europe absorbed the valuable products of Islamic culture (e.g. in mathematics) whilst still despising the 'barbarian'. So also did China which added the riches of Buddhist and other cultures whilst maintaining cultural chauvinism. Both civilisations remained, in their own eyes, the centre of the world. In both cultures there was a significant development of science and technology (with China doing much better than Europe at least until the eighteenth century) yet a linear view of history necessary to a theory of modernisation remained absent. The dominant view was cyclical and the only alternative was millenarian revolt.

Yet, in the West, the seventeenth century saw the beginnings of a fundamental change. The discovery (or invention) of the 'individual' as a political actor needed a new theory of political obligation. For Aristotle, who in Hobbes's day was still required reading in most western universities, the fundamental political unit was the politically-determined citizen not the pre-social individual with rights independent of society. For the early Christians what was pre-social was the human soul. This belief was reconciled with the Aristotelian view by St. Thomas Aquinas and it was not until the seventeenth century that the state came to be interpreted as a mechanism to preserve pre-social human rights, namely life, liberty and estate. There is much argument about what brought about this change. But all agree it was the product of revolution. For crude Marxists it was essentially the product of the early bourgeois revolution which demanded a theory which would legitimise the pursuit of individual wealth whilst discouraging expenditure. The 'Protestant ethic', therefore, was a way of maximising investment so necessary to primitive capitalist accumulation. At the same time individualism broke down affective ties (kinship etc.), making for a transferable labour force. Others, however, in the Weberian tradition, argue that two revolutions proceeded simultaneously. The first of these, the Puritan revolution (what we have referred to earlier as a cultural revolution), antedated the bourgeois revolution but provided a behavioural disposition which was able to serve the ends of capital accumulation. In other words the bourgeois (political-economic) revolution did not cause the cultural revolution, nor was the reverse the case; what occurred was a happy coincidence.

In both of these views there is an element of ethnocentricity. There are many ways whereby savings may become investment, and a market orientation may be fostered other than by developing a theory of individual human rights. One has only to look at the history of Song China (960-1280), or for that matter Chinese communities in Asia in more recent times, to document that. It is true that capitalism (in the Marxian sense of a mode of production which had at its core a class which had nothing to sell but its labour power and a ruling class which lived off surplus value) did not develop in China until after the impact of the West. But then neither did it develop in Europe until at least a century after the doctrine of individual human rights was put forward. One suspects that the crude Marxist view results from a projection backwards from the Britain described in Marx's Capital. Because Britain was the most advanced capitalist country in the mid-nineteenth century, then surely it had been further on the way towards developing capitalist ideas in the seventeenth century. Such might be the case but it is not necessarily so, and the answer can only be reached by an exercise in comparative economic history. As for the Weberian view, it has to be demonstrated why the orientation towards investment was more likely to follow from the Puritan cultural revolution than any other change in ideas in the seventeenth century. Indeed the Catholic ideas promoted in the cities of the Italian Renaissance were equally conducive to productive investment.

By casting 'modern' society in terms of that capitalist behaviour which has pertained in England and Northern Europe since the Industrial Revolution the views of the seventeenth century discussed above may be seen as ethnocentric. They focus on revolution in two of the senses outlined in our Introduction. What may be said about the seventeenth century in terms of the third narrowly political definition to which we have referred? The English revolution of mid-century was certainly quite violent and did result in a lasting change of regime; this is quite clear when one considers that the attempts to restore the status quo ante in the reigns of Charles II and James II were to result in the relatively non-violent 'revolution' of 1688. That revolution was celebrated as the successful reconciliation of the essence of natural law based on pre-social human rights with a social contract establishing a sovereign to which all owed obedience. At the core of the system was a process of representation and the institutions of limited government. It was as if 1688 was the summit of human history, and accordingly generations of Whig historians rewrote history to show why the historical developments of preceding centuries all pointed to the Whig achievement. At first the 'glorious revolution' of 1688 was seen as largely an English affair but, within a century, it was seen as having universal application. Despite his comments on the specificity of national traditions, this was the model which the French theorist Montesquieu took as epitomising a 'balance of powers' (legislative executive and judiciary) which might be emulated by other countries.[8] In fact, Montesquieu's picture of England was not a particularly accurate one and it is probably fair to say that he was constructing what Max Weber would call an 'ideal type'[9] rather than a historical description. Nevertheless the point needs to be made; Montesquieu was engaged in what political scientists of the 1950s and 1960s called the study of 'political development'.

Such an exercise is perhaps the most ethnocentric of all. The procedure is to establish a model of what a developed polity looks like and then to show how other polities diverge from it and what they need to do to 'catch up'. In the 1950s the models which were created looked suspiciously like the United States though some of the more unsavoury elements of American political life might be dispensed with and replaced by features of an idealised Britain. But it was not only the Americans and Britons who engaged in this ethnocentric exercise. Soviet writers also were at pains to show their satellites and clients a glimpse of their political future. Sometimes, however, the ethnocentric model-building approach became curiously inverted and the political model of the future was cast as an idealised China. Such a practice, common amongst radical groups in the 1960s, can be traced back to the mid-seventeenth century when the philosophes of the Englightenment looked with envy on a (mythical) Chinese model of administrative rationality with which to contrast the despotism (enlightened or otherwise) which characterised European countries at that time.

Leaving aside the construction of inverted political models, a few conclusions might now be made about the normal ethnocentric approach to political development and the role of revolution in its narrowly political definition. Amongst the practitioners of the ethnocentric approach there is usually an affirmation and an idealisation of the political revolution which brought the system into being, be it the 'glorious revolution' of 1688 or the American revolution after 1776. In the West, however, most people believe that the realisation of that model by other countries must be pursued by non-revolutionary means. In the Soviet Union, on the other hand, the idealisation of the Bolshevik revolution is joined to the belief that other countries will have to go through a similar political upheaval. But woe betide any which attempts to do without Soviet guidance. The relatively independent revolutions in China and Yugoslavia have not fared well amongst Soviet commentators. At least that is how the situation used to be. Since the 1960s new elements have entered Soviet thought about the

---

8.   C. Montesquieu, The Spirit of the Laws, revised edn., 2 vols, Hafner, New York, 1965.

9.   Weber defines an 'ideal type' as 'the synthesis of a great many diffuse, discrete, more or less present and occasionally absent concrete individual phenomena which are arranged according to...one-sidedly emphasised viewpoints into a unified analytical construct'; M. Weber, '"Objectivity" in Social Science and Social Policy', in M. Weber, The Methodology of the Social Sciences, Free Press, New York, 1949, p.90.

process of development and the notion of a 'non-capitalist path to development', prescribed for India, might suggest that theoretically (though certainly not strategically) the Soviet ideologists are moving closer to a multilinear view of political development.

We have so far looked at ethnocentric interpretations of modernisation and revolution in all three senses outlined earlier. In each case the spread of what is considered to be modernity is by <u>diffusion</u>. The Roman Empire and the Han Empire achieved this largely at the point of a sword. After their collapse, the superior (Roman and Han) values were kept alive by a clerical (or mandarin) establishment which eventually was able to civilise the 'barbarians' and develop the original culture to new heights. The ideas of the seventeenth century liberals spread along with the capitalist mode of production; or if one prefers the reverse scenario, the Puritan ethic produced its own missionaries who converted secular rulers eager to achieve independence from outside authority. The Whig tradition eventually followed the British flag to all corners of the globe and its American version followed the military advisers and the dollar. Similarly the Soviet model was actively promoted by its agents or developed in the wake of its armies.

For the west, at least, cultural diffusion provided an explanation as to why revolution was unnecessary to development. We shall discuss in the next chapter the response of the third world to such a view. In the meantime we must note that the consequence was to see the majority of countries in the world as in a static state of 'traditional' equilibrium, until the advent of the particular package of prescribed 'modern' ideas reached them. Thus some British anthropologists of the 1930s could affirm the conservative faith in the equal worth of all 'traditional' cultures and bemoan the consequences of the inevitable march of progress. Yet the conditions under which their research had become possible were created by a process of diffusion which would destroy the cultures they were studying. Often their own researches contributed to that end.

The Multilinear View

Diffusionist theories, it would seem, suggest that all societies in the world are converging towards a common model. Differences between societies are explained in terms of the level of economic development, the rate of social change necessary to 'catch up' and the 'late development effect' (where 'advanced' technology is imported into backward societies allowing them to bypass certain stages of development). But are such explanations adequate? Were there any 'traditional' static societies which only changed due to outside stimuli and to which revolution was exported? Indeed it is probably the case that most societies contain within them potentialities for radical change and that those potentialities differ according to historical and geographical conditions. In other words there could be a number of different routes to a number of different types of modernisation and that in each of these routes there were potentialities for different types of revolution.

A superficial reading of the official Soviet Marxist-Leninist canon would lead one to the conclusion that Karl Marx and Friedrich Engels saw progress in a unilinear sense. Primitive communism gave way to ancient society. That in turn developed into feudalism which gave way to capitalism and eventually communism. Each transition from one type of society to another was the result of an internal dynamic (the clash between the productive forces and the relations of production in the dominant mode of production) and constituted a revolution in the political economy sense of the word. But such a neat picture does not accord with Marx and Engels' writings. They were both good enough historians to realise that very different types of society had developed in different parts of the world and that the principle of internal causation led to the possibility of different routes to modernisation. To be sure, Marx and Engels believed that, by the nineteenth century, the capitalist mode of production was spreading throughout the world, but the process of diffusion was new and was specific to capitalism. In the past the principle of diffusion was insufficient to explain social change and one had to consider a number of different routes to modernity specified by the different contradictions in various types of society.

Marx and Engels' starting point was primitive communism. The division of labour which developed under that system with the increase in population and communal needs might result in three different forms of society:

1. the ancient form
2. the Germanic form
3. the Asiatic form with its Slavonic sub-type.

The first of these, the ancient (Greek and Roman) form, came into existence after tribal society, hitherto divided only on the basis of kinship, developed distinctions between chieftains and the rest of the population. An elaborate division of labour, resulting from increased population and the development of external relations, gave rise to problems which were solved by the institution of slavery.[10] Slavery was to become one of the prime identifying characteristics of ancient society; it provided a dynamic for economic growth but, at the same time, its institutional form imposed limits on that growth. Ancient society was dominated by the cities yet those cities depended upon agriculture. The Roman citizen was essentially a landowner oriented towards the city as the centre of co-operation for the communal labour of war. The expansion of ancient society consisted in the use of armies to enlarge the landed estates of the Roman citizens and consequently to extend the system of slavery and the growth of a monetary economy beyond the cities.[11] The expansion of such a system depended upon the degree to which military force was able to subdue the rural subsistence economy which had also developed out of primitive communism. In its Germanic form the rural division of labour had not broken away from communal forms of organisation and property. But the Germanic form was not static. The commune consisted of more than a collectivity of self-sustaining peasants, its leaders being able to mobilise surplus labour time for the pursuit of war. Increasingly that war was

---

10. Karl Marx and Friedrich Engels, The German Ideology (1845-6) Chapter 1, reproduced in part in Marx and Engels, Pre-Capitalist Economic Formations, Progress Publishers, Moscow, 1979; see also Introduction by E.J. Hobsbawm, Karl Marx, Pre-Capitalist Economic Formations, International Publishers, New York, 1965.

11. Hobsbawm, op.cit., p. 74.

directed against the inroads made by the Roman system of slavery and, in the end, was able to engulf the cities and the commercial and cultural life within them. The argument here needs to be stressed. Feudalism was certainly a consequence of the breakdown of the Roman military and commercial system, but its dynamic derived from an alternative path of development which had existed right through the centuries of the Roman Empire. Revolution, in the political economy sense of the word, was the necessary consequence of the clash of two forms of social organisation. These existed in the ancient form but were centred on different parts of society, one in the cities and one in the country; they were located also in different parts of the Empire, one in the metropoles and the other in the periphery. Current arguments about the tensions of the 'world system' have a long history.

Rejecting the 'unilinear' reading of Marx and Engels, we have argued that they, in fact, saw feudalism as an alternative path of development which stemmed from Germanic tribal society. Its origins were much wider than the bounds of the Roman Empire and consequently it was able to develop also in areas never occupied by the Romans. What changed with the decline of Rome was that communal property gradually became the property of feudal lords who were backed by the military might of the Germanic conquerors of Rome. With such a development, slavery disappeared since, under the Romans, it had been an urban-based form; as such it was antithetical to the new dominant rural-based economy. Slaves were actually owned by a master. Now there developed a new class of serfs who were not directly owned by a lord. The lord owned not the serfs but the land to which they were tied.[12]

The new rural-orientation of society meant that urban development was sharply separated from what went on in the countryside. In the cities, individual craftsmen organised themselves into guilds of master craftsmen which commanded the labour of journeymen and apprentices. When runaway serfs entered the towns they were required either to work as unskilled labourers with no power, or to be 'bent to the will' of the guild-masters. Since towns were relatively isolated and migration from the rural areas was sporadic, the acts of insubordination on the part of journeymen and apprentices and the occasional revolts of day labourers were never able to develop revolutionary potential in either the political economy sense or in the sense of challenging the regime of any feudal lord. In the Middle Ages 'the great risings all radiated from the countryside'. Yet even these risings, Marx and Engels felt, were ineffective due to the isolated life of peasants which inhibited the development of class consciousness. Faced with the organised power of the princes and nobility, the peasants had no hope of effecting significant change except in alliance with one of the other estates. In the meantime the peasants were exploited by each of them.[13] All there could be was resignation punctuated by the occasional jacquerie (spontaneous revolt).

The revolutionary transition from the ancient form to the feudal form according to Marx and Engels, it will be remembered, was the consequence of a contradiction between two principles of social organisation which

---

12. Marx and Engels, op.cit., pp. 39-45.

13. ibid., pp. 64-5.

existed right through the life of ancient Rome. That contradiction matured to the extent that urban life was separated from rural life, and indeed the Empire was brought down by the invasions of people who had never known the pax Romana of the cities. Similarly Marx and Engels saw the feudal form being brought to an end by the contradiction between two principles of social organisation which existed throughout the life of the feudal form. This was once again the contradiction between town and country. The separation of town and country under feudalism divided capital from landed property and urban labourers from the land to which they had once been tied. The town burghers, organised for the defence of their commercial interests against landowners, provided the nucleus of what was termed a bourgeoisie. The political-economic revolution which ensued shifted the developmental focus back once again to the towns and carried on the process begun under the ancient form. This time, however, bourgeois leadership brought about the commercialisation of agriculture which no longer required the military domination of the countryside. At the same time 'free labour' had replaced slavery. Under slavery the slaves were totally owned by the slave owner. Under feudalism the serfs were free to provide their own subsistence but were tied to land owned by a lord. Now the workers were legally free to choose to whom to sell their 'labour power'. But over that labour power they surrendered control for the length of the working day. In many ways the loss of autonomy was greater than under feudalism but was legitimised by the workers' right to choose between employers or to choose not to work and to starve.

The above route to (capitalist) modernity, portrayed by Marx and Engels is, we have argued, a synthesis of two principles of organisation centred on the one hand on the cities and on the other on the countryside. Both the ancient form and the feudal form rested on the separation of city and countryside and the demise of both resulted in large measure from an exacerbation of that separation. The third alternative discussed by Marx is much more controversial. This is the oriental route, sometimes referred to as 'The Asiatic Mode of Production'. Here there was no separation of city and countryside. At most there was, according to Marx, merely the 'self sustaining unity of manufacture and agriculture within a village commune that contains within itself all the conditions for reproduction and surplus production'. This, however, was not the same as the Germanic commune which acquired a dynamism of its own in resisting the encroachments made on land by the Roman cities and thus acted as a spur to feudalism. On the contrary, the Asiatic cities were not the loci of alternative principles of organisation which attempted to impose, at first, slavery, and then a free labour market upon the countryside. They were rather creatures of a despotic state which only related to the village communities in its desire to ensure taxation and forced labour to maintain hydraulic (water transport/irrigation) and communication works. The cities were the result of a parasitic state structure.[14]

At various times in his life, Marx oscillated between two very different views on 'Asiatic' society. Each of these views had very different implications for the degree to which such societies could change and the possibilities for revolution. The first of these views was set out in his Grundrisse (1858). Here Marx argued that the state ownership of land,

---

14.   See Hobsbawm, op.cit., pp. 33-36.

which was felt by many of his contemporaries to be the defining feature of Asiatic society, was in fact only an ideological mask. While centralised despotic states stood above the village communities, appearing as the higher or sole proprietors with the real communities appearing only as hereditary possessors, in reality the self-sufficient village communities were based on tribal communal ownership. As long as the 'oriental despot', commonly portrayed as the 'father' of the people, received his taxes and his forced labour. (corvee) drafts, the village communities were unaffected by any formal legal principles which governed land ownership. Those communities might take one of two forms. They might 'vegetate independently side by side with the individual in his community labouring with his family on the land allotted to them' or they could participate in a communal form of land organisation. In the former instance a certain amount of labour within the village had to be contributed to the common store (for war, religious worship etc.) and this could give rise to a primitive form of feudalism where the power of local lords arose out of control of that surplus labour (as in Slavonic or Romanian communities). In the latter instance, feudalism was precluded.[15] The implications of Marx's argument are profound. Marx seems to be saying that an 'Asiatic' form of society based on communal ownership might bypass the feudal phase of development. Could one adhere to Marx's views about the necessary sequence of modes of production and yet argue that the Asiatic mode might bypass capitalism?

Unfortunately Marx did not explore the implications in his Grundrisse argument. In his more mature work, Capital, the first volume of which appeared in 1867, Marx set aside his notion about communal ownership in the oriental village in preference for the more orthodox thesis that the sovereignty of the state was based on ownership of the land concentrated on a national scale. He accepted also the conventional wisdom that Asiatic societies were unchangeable entities in which the direct producer was subordinated to the state and where rent and taxes coincided. Finally he adopted another common view which held that it was the rulers' need to maintain huge hydraulic works in agriculture which provided the basis for the absence of private property. This was what made the East different from the West.[16]

The above two views had clearly different implications for revolution. The Grundrisse view implied that a revolution might occur in Asiatic society which would be quite unlike anything which Marx depicted or foresaw in the west. The Capital view, on the other hand, suggested that Asiatic societies were totally stagnant.[17] Revolution would only come to them as a result of a foreign invasion which would import forms of

---

15.   P. Anderson, Lineages of the Absolutist State, New Left Books, London, 1974, pp. 477-478. Also see E. Hobsbawm, op.cit., pp. 69-71.

16.   P. Anderson, op.cit. (p. 477) notes that this analysis was 'in effect, the fusion of three themes that had hitherto been relatively distinct - hydraulic agriculture (Smith), geographical destiny (Montesquieu), and state agrarian property (Bernier)'.

17.   See Anderson, op.cit., pp. 480-481.

production from the west. This is not merely an esoteric academic point. Revolutions in the name of Marx did occur in Russia and China and scholars are locked in debate as to the influence of foreign powers and the extent to which traditional forms of organisation may have persisted within them. The revolutionaries in Russia and China did not have the Grundrisse as a guide, but they were aware of Marx's reversion to the Grundrisse view in his comments of 1881. Here Marx argued more explicitly that the Russian village community, the obstchina, was one in which property in land was communal. The Russian state, moreover, was described as a parasitical growth which, once overthrown, could allow for capitalism to be bypassed in Russia.[18] The Capital view, however, that this would depend on proletarian revolution elsewhere in the world, was maintained. As we know Lenin was not particularly influenced by Marx's 1881 views. Nor indeed, in our opinion, should he have been. If the Russian obstchina was ever very significant, it had long since ceased to be so by the time of the Bolshevik Revolution. In China, moreover, the idea of communal ownership of property had not existed for many centuries, if indeed it ever was significant. In our view, the Asiatic Mode of Production is empirically and theoretically rather vacuous. It is discussed here merely because it has informed and continues to inform a large body of literature on comparative history. Whilst rejecting the Asiatic Mode, however, we do not subscribe to a unilinear view of history. A multilinear view of history seems to be essential and it is significant that many writers in this genre follow the work of Marx.

As was noted previously, the unlinear view of history which now informs the official Marxist-Leninist position in the Soviet Union owes much to the work of Josef Stalin who was to purge the Asiatic Mode of Production from the official Marxist canon. A famous refutation of Stalin might be found in the work of Karl August Wittfogel whose Oriental Despotism[19] still remains influential in many university courses in sociology. Starting from the view that the west was characterised by 'equilibrated pluralism' and the east by Stalinist dictatorship, Wittfogel located the crucial historical difference in the fact that the east never escaped from the Asiatic Mode. This continued to manifest itself as 'oriental despotism' in contrast to the west's transition through feudalism to bourgeois democracy. Following Marx's description in Capital, Wittfogel argued that the east could not escape because of the importance of a strong bureaucratic state to maintain massive hydraulic works. In the west, however, small states could develop which allowed for a much greater degree of popular control over government. Revolutions were common to both types of society. In the east, however, they succeed only in producing a more centralised dictatorship whereas in the west they facilitated the end of feudalism and absolutism. If one applies the typology outlined in our Introduction, one may conclude that Wittfogel is arguing that revolutions in the east were only of the third narrowly political type whilst in the west such revolutions contributed to revolutions which were

---

18.   See Marx, second draft of a letter to Zasulich (March, 1881), quoted in Hobsbawm, op.cit., pp. 142-144.

19.   K. Wittfogel, Oriental Despotism: A Comparative Study of Total Power, Yale University Press, New Haven, 1957.

both political-economic and cultural. Wittfogel's approach has been challenged on many grounds, the most important of which is his use of the Asiatic Mode of Production premised on the non-private ownership of land. As the critics of Marx's thesis have pointed out, such a mode rarely existed in the past and thus is not very useful in explaining the situation now.[20] Finally and perhaps most important of all, Wittfogel provides us with a classic example of what happens when one extrapolates from the present. There can be no alternatives other than the ones which already exist. Wittfogel's conclusion is none other than his initial assumption.

A much more stimulating account of multilinear development was provided by Barrington Moore in his Social Origins of Dictatorship and Democracy.[21] This study projected backwards from three end states - bourgeois democracy, fascism and communism and dealt with the relationship of revolution in the narrow political sense to revolution in the political economic sense. Modernity, for Moore, was promoted by the development of market relations in agriculture within a rational centralised state. Unlike many other studies his focus was not simply on the groups which carried out a successful revolution but on the relationship of those groups to the classes which were seen to have been crowded off the face of history - in particular the peasantry. Having noted 'the curious fact' that by the sixteenth and seventeenth centuries royal absolutist states or agrarian bureaucracies had been established in all the major countries he studied (England, France, the Prussian part of Germany, Russia, China, Japan and India) Moore approached the question: were there structural features which may be identified in agrarian societies which facilitated, hindered or even made impossible the development of parliamentary democracy? Moore concluded that Western feudalism contained certain conditions which distinguished it from other societies. It was only in Western Europe that a delicate balance occurred between too much and too little royal power. In the west (unlike Russia) there was no need for an Ivan the Terrible to break the back of the independent nobility, nor was there a central authority supervising the activities of the society as a whole.[22] For Moore the first route to modernity - that of bourgeois revolution - was traversed in England, France, and in the United States. In pursuing revolution in the wider (political economy) sense, each of those countries went through a bloody revolution in the narrow political sense. In England this was the Puritan Revolution of the mid-seventeenth century. In France it was the Great Revolution of 1789-95 and in the United States it was the Civil War of 1861-65. In each case a strong bourgeoisie was able to rise to power. Its choice of allies, however, determined the nature, scope and direction of violence.

In England, the bourgeoisie allied itself with a sizeable section of the landed gentry to oppose an absolutist monarch who was concerned to

---

20.   For an informative critique of the 'Asiatic mode', see Anderson, op.cit., pp. 484-495.

21.   Barrington Moore Jr., Social Origins of Dictatorship and Democracy: Lord and Peasant in the Making of the Modern World, Beacon Press, Boston, 1966.

22.   See Moore, op.cit., p. 415.

prevent the destruction of the peasantry as a class. The victory of this alliance against Charles I in the Civil War was seen by Moore to have hastened the destruction of the peasantry. This was a key element in agricultural modernity since it enabled England to adopt a commercial form of agriculture which linked up town and country in a system of complementary markets. At the same time the 'eliminated' peasantry could be absorbed into a completely new kind of social formation.

The landed upper classes had split in their attitude towards the policies of Charles I, in particular with regard to the peasants. The elimination of the peasantry, however, did not lead to a unified reassertion of landed interests. On the contrary, the post-Civil War period was characterised by the continuation of shifting coalitions between various groups of landed interests and the urban bourgeoisie. This provided the basic framework for interest group politics characteristic of bourgeois parliamentary democracy. Moreover, with the defeat of royal absolutism and with the peasantry on the way to destruction there was no need for a strong state to maintain the extraction of the agricultural surplus.[23]

In France, on the other hand, the landed gentry resisted the commercialisation of agriculture and opposed the bourgeoisie. The bourgeoisie, therefore, sought allies amongst the peasantry to overthrow the ancien regime. The result was the bloody revolution of 1789-95 which destroyed the landed gentry and left the bourgeoisie and the peasantry holding the field. The identity of interest between those classes was sufficiently great to allow for a bourgeois democracy but not great enough to allow for the same kind of weak state structure as England. There remained problems of extracting the agricultural surplus and the peasants, fearing for their survival, were given to political extremes which from time to time threatened the stability of the new regime. In short, the result was an unstable bourgeois democracy.

In the United States two types of economy existed in two different parts of the country. Neither the north nor the south possessed a peasantry. In the north there was a class of independent farmers already assimilated into commercialised agriculture with no conflict of interest with the bourgeoisie. In the south there was, of course, a landed gentry and slaves working in a plantation economy which had been commercialised along lines completely different to the north. The clash was to occur over which kind of economic system would dominate the newly opened west. The result was a protracted period of violence which took the form of a civil war between regions. This civil war, Moore considered, constituted a revolution more profound than that commenced in 1776. The outcome was the destruction of the landed gentry as a class and the freeing of the slaves. Since there was no major conflict of interest between the dominant classes in the north - the bourgeoisie and the independent farmers - bourgeois democracy prevailed and there was no need for a strong state to extract the agricultural surplus.

The second route from pre-industrial society to modernity was, according to Moore, exemplified by Germany. Here the bourgeoisie was much weaker than in the west. For such a bourgeoisie to challenge the landed gentry would be to invite disaster. Consequently sections of the relatively weak commercial and industrial bourgeoisie sought dissident

---

23.   ibid., pp. 423-424.

elements of the dominant landed gentry to put through the changes required for industrial society. For basically military reasons it was possible to find such elements and this fraction of the landed gentry took the initiative in promoting the development of industry and the commercialisation of agriculture.

There was, however, a clash of interests between, on the one hand, the dominant allies which tried to maximise the extraction of the rural surplus and, on the other, a peasantry which feared for its future. Instead of surplus extraction through the market which aided the development of parliamentary democracy in the west, a labour repressive agrarian system grew up which depended on political mechanisms (and here the term is used very loosely) to ensure that a large number of people worked the land to provide a surplus to be consumed by other classes. The route to parliamentary democracy, as experienced in the west, was blocked in Prussia when the Prussian nobility expanded its holdings at the expense of the peasantry, just as that class was about to be emancipated under the Teutonic Order. Together with the reduction of the peasantry to a new form of serfdom, a process was initiated where towns were reduced to dependence upon the rural-based nobility by curtailing the export of their products in favour of the direct export of agricultural produce in the form of grain. The throttling of the market between town and country was to inhibit any alliance between landowners and townspeople and this was further exacerbated by the Hohenzollern policy of destroying the independence of the nobility and playing off nobles and bourgeoisie one against the other. Consequently, rather than strong parliamentary democracy, there took shape the militarised fusion of bureaucracy and landed aristocracy which was to take the initiative in the modernisation process. The parliamentary forms which did develop in Germany were never strong enough to solve the economic and social problems which confronted them. Upon their collapse, the peasants were dealt with by a mixture of repression and mobilisation behind symbols which stemmed from a rural tradition. This process culminated in fascism or 'revolution from above'.[24]

The Japanese sub-alternative to the above model was also to result in a 'total commitment to authority' and, like Prussia, the fascist route was initiated once a weak industrial and commercial bourgeoisie sought elements of the landed classes to take the lead in the process of industrial-isation.[25] But where such a situation was impossible, either because the bourgeoisie was too weak or suitable allies in the dominant class could not be found, the result was not fascism but a 'peasant revolution' leading to communism. Such, Moore tells us, is what happened in Russia and China. This was his third route to modernisation.[26]

In Russia and China, society was dominated by a huge agrarian bureaucracy which served to inhibit the impulse to modernisation more than in any of the countries discussed so far. Yet even Russia and China were not insulated from modernisation in other countries and foreign

---

24. ibid., pp, 434-5 and pp. 460-8.

25. ibid., p. 436.

26. ibid., p 437.

influence began to be felt in parts of the two empires. Such influence produced strains amongst the peasantry which was to provide the main force for overthrowing the old order under the leadership of Communist parties. The key to the effectiveness of peasant revolution in those countries was to be found in the way the agricultural surplus was extracted. Again the western pattern of extracting the rural surplus through the market was absent. The extraction of the surplus in Russia and China depended upon the power of the centralised agrarian bureaucracy. In the west the power of the central government was not particularly relevant to the peasants, whereas in Russia and China the peasants were conscious of the fact that the strength of the central government affected directly the amount of the agricultural surplus they had to surrender. In such a situation they had a strong motivation to overthrow the agrarian bureaucracy.

The peasant revolutions of recent times changed fundamentally the idea of the peasant as merely an object of history, as 'a form of social life over which historical changes pass but which contributes nothing to the impetus of those changes'. But here there is a cruel irony! At the point in Moore's account where the peasantry became a major element in historical change, it ceased to exist as a class. The peasantry which made revolution has in every case become its major victim. In Russia and China, collectivisation has been carried on by a state made even stronger than before in order to maximise the rural surplus. This has spelt doom to the peasants as a class.[27]

Immediately upon its publication in the mid-1960s, Moore's book was greeted with much acclaim amongst social theorists and a barrage of criticism from historians of each of the countries he discussed.[28] It was pointed out that the English peasantry took a long time to disappear and that the English Civil War could hardly be considered part of the 'bourgeois revolution'. As for France, many historians refused to accept that France before 1789 was feudal at all. Similarly historians of Germany and Japan confronted Moore with their objections. Most damning was criticism of Moore's adoption of fascism as the end state of German and Japanese development; just what, it was asked, has been going on since 1945?

---

27.   ibid., p. 453.

28.   See S. Rothman, 'Barrington Moore and the Dialectics of Revolution', American Political Science Review 64, March 1970, pp. 61-85, 182-3; T. Tilton, 'The Social Origin of Liberal Democracy: The Swedish Case', American Political Science Review 68, June 1974, pp. 561-71; T. Skopcol, 'A Critical Review of Barrington Moore's Social Origins of Dictatorship and Democracy', Politics and Society; Vol. IV, No. 1, Fall 1973, pp. 1-34; D. Lowenthal, review in History and Theory, Vol VII, No. 2, 1968, pp. 257-78; J.V. Femia, 'Barrington Moore and the Pre-conditions for Democracy', British Journal of Political Science, Vol. II, No. 2, pp. 21-46; L. Stone, 'News from Everywhere', New York Review of Books, Vol. IX, 24 August 1967, pp. 31-5; R. Dore, 'Making Sense of History', Archives Europeenes de Sociologie, Vol. X, 1969, pp. 295-305; J. Weiner, 'The Barrington Moore Thesis and its Critics', Theory and Society, 2, 1975, pp. 301-30.

Others could not see how the Russian revolution could be described as 'peasant'. Doubtless more peasants took part than any other class but that was also true of the English revolution. Moore's answer was that one should define a revolution not in terms of who takes part nor in terms of its leaders but in terms of the interests served (which is how he characterises the 'bourgeois revolutions' in England and France). But if that is the case and if it is true that the peasants have been destroyed as a class, was either the Russian or the Chinese revolutions 'peasant'? In any case it is extraordinarily difficult to argue that the peasants in Russia and China have disappeared as classes except in the sense of becoming kolkhoz (collective farm) workers or commune members who as individuals no longer legally own most of the land.

A further set of criticisms centre on the universality which Moore claims for his scheme. Having outlined his typology, Moore then attempts to see how one may deal with India. The results are inconclusive. What, one wonders, would he do with Switzerland and Sweden? An appeal to the old diffusionist viewpoint that smaller countries follow large ones ignores the fact that those two countries were more autonomous than Germany at the time of its unification.

In short, Moore's argument is open to various criticisms. For all that, his study is one of the most stimulating in the multilinear genre, giving us very useful insights into the type of violence employed in the various countries he studied. Whether the main task of relating revolution in the narrowly political sense to revolution in the political-economic sense succeeds is an open question but one may profit much by his discussion of revolution in the first sense.

Moore's criterion of modernisation - the development of market relations in agriculture in a rational centralised state which in turn promotes the rise of bourgeois democratic institutions - leaves him open to the charge of ethnocentricity. It is true that market relations have developed in all the societies he considers but, it might be argued, the development of market relations in Eastern Europe, the Soviet Union and China are of a kind qualitatively different from those in Western Europe and the United States. Moreover, we believe that the weakness of Moore's argument lies in the inconsistency in his methodology. Having focussed on the commercialisation of agriculture, Moore has investigated the development of a strong bourgeoisie in the west and has gone from that to explain the attendant development of a durable parliamentary democracy. But, when investigating the east, Moore has not convincingly explored the conditions under which a strong bourgeoisie failed to develop nor to examine the consequences of that failure. One attempt to answer that question so vital to the modernisation process 'East of the Elbe' is provided by a recent work, The Intellectuals on the Road to Class Power by the Hungarian scholars Georgy Konrad and Ivan Szelenyi.[29]

The Intellectuals on the Road to Class Power consists of an attempt to combine the approaches of Karl Marx and the Austrian theorist

---

29.   G. Konrad and I. Szelenyi, The Intellectuals on the Road to Class Power: A Sociological Study of the Role of the Intelligentsia in Socialism, Harcourt, Brace and Jovanovich, New York, 1979.

Karl Polanyi.[30] Polanyi's starting point was not so much the Marxian concept of mode of production but the way in which various national economic systems were <u>integrated</u>. Of the four ways of integrating an economy which Polanyi described, two are important for the analysis of Konrad and Szelenyi - market integration (of the west) and redistributive integration (of the east).

In describing the development of market integration in the west, Konrad and Szelenyi differ little from the account provided by Marx. What is original in their approach is their focus on the development of a stratum they call intellectual, i.e. those whose position is legitimised by a knowledge of the 'laws of society'. The intellectuals in the west constitute a stratum rather than a class in the Marxist sense because they belong strictly neither to the capitalist class nor to the proletariat. They resemble proletarians, we are told, because they sell their labour power in the same way as the workers.[31] At the same time, however, significant groups of intellectuals have been able to control the price of their labour (through the creation of monopolies) and under such a situation one may speak of the existence of intellectual capital. The western intellectuals, therefore, have been pulled in two directions, leading to a situation where different parts of the intellectual stratum might fuse with proletariat or bourgeoisie.

With the development of capitalism, the debasement of intellectual values by the operation of the market led to a tendency for many intellectuals to legitimise themselves in terms of a <u>telos</u> (mission). Thus the Jacobin intellectuals of the French Revolution legitimised their actions by reference to the rights and interests of the 'people', whereas in fact they served the real interests of the bourgeoisie. Similar intellectuals, who like the French lawyers could command a high price for their labour in the years which followed, attempted to synthesise their <u>telos</u> with an acceptance of the capitalist labour market. On the other hand, different groups of intellectuals, fearing proletarianisation, expressed their teleological mission as a rejection of capitalism and an affirmation of alliance with the working class. The result of all this was the inability of intellectuals, split by the labour market, to develop beyond an intermediate stratum and to proceed towards class power (i.e. power over the means of production and the mechanisms of distribution). Such a situation might be expected to remain as long as the two legitimising principles of capital ownership and a technocratically defined mission remain of equal importance in a market-integrated economy.

---

30.   K. Polanyi, <u>The Great Transformation: The Political and Economic Origins of Our Time</u> (1944), Beacon Books, Boston, 1957.

31.   This conclusion is highly questionable, in Marxist terms, in that what is usually sold is not labour power (alienated labour) but labour (over which the seller maintains a significant degree of control). Nevertheless there is evidence to support Konrad and Szelenyi's view that what has been occurring in capitalist society is a general proletarianisation of intellectuals (a proposition which may be cast in Marxist language as the transformation of labour into labour power).

18.

Though Konrad and Szelenyi do not explore the implications of such an analysis for the process of revolution, it is possible to make a few observations consistent with their analysis. The eighteenth century Enlightenment, it might be said, had two results. By removing feudal obstacles it was able to further the development of capitalism and market integration. At the same time its fostering of rationality provided a telos for the liberated intellectual. Revolution in the cultural sense then gave rise to revolution in the narrowly political sense. The consequence of the revolutionary upheavals was a split in the ranks of the new intellectuals, between those who wanted to be in a position to realise their telos and those who were content to sell their services to the highest bidder on the intellectual labour market. This split has persisted ever since. Those intellectuals who chose to identify with the working class were always in a weak position, since a significant proportion of them could always be persuaded to profit by their intellectual capital on the labour market. They were thus incorporated into social-democratic parties which continued to play by the rules of a market-integrated economy. Western political life was not conducive to revolution in the narrow political sense. It was possible to argue, however, that the growth of a new form of capitalism dominated by huge corporations provided significant opportunities for a group of intellectuals to rise to power on the basis of a new managerial telos though, up to the present, the strength of the legitimising ideology of capital ownership has prevented such a development.

The story was completely different in Eastern Europe and Russia. Like Moore, Konrad and Szelenyi begin by noting that the economy of that region was never fully integrated by the market. The basic form of intergration which has prevailed over the past few centuries is redistributive (where the central government appropriates the bulk of the economic surplus and determines its distribution by administrative means): a mode of redistributive integration that Konrad and Szelenyi date from around the twelfth century. At that time, the society of the east was not significantly different from that of the west; it was simply poorer. But the Mongul, Tartar and Turkish invasions introduced elements of what Marx called the 'Asiatic Mode of Production'. A redistributive system was set up, not to maintain hydraulic works (the centrepiece of Wittfogel's analysis) but to develop large standing armies. The decline of 'Asiatic' power was to result less in the development of market relations and more in an adaptation of the 'Asiatic Mode' by local rulers. In Russia during the reigns of Ivan the Great, Ivan the Terrible and Peter the Great, the power of the hereditary nobility was broken and what there was of a patrimonial system (where landholding was based on heredity) gave way to a prebendal system (where the usufruct of state lands was handed over to a service nobility only so long as it maintained office). The members of this service nobility could be transferred to different parts of the empire on military service or to collect taxes, with the result that they could not stay on their estates to develop agriculture. The transformation of the military role to that of tax collector in villages with which they had no traditional identification led to government officials simply extracting as high a proportion of the surplus as they could. In short, 'they practised a predatory economy'. Such a situation prevented more intensive methods of agricultural cultivation and, instead of developing skills, the peasants were driven back to a form of serfdom which had prevailed under Tartar rule. Like Moore, Konrad and Szelenyi note that in this context there was no use for a skilled agricultural labour force. The chief concern of the Russian nobility was to secure an adequate supply of servile labour. Such was the origin of what became known as the 'second serfdom'.

In the western parts of the land east of the Elbe, a degree of market orientation had developed under the influence of Roman law. Once the payment of tax in kind had replaced labour service as a feudal obligation to the lord, peasants had some incentive to invest and expand production. But the advent of 'second serfdom', reversed this process. Village communities were reduced to a process of simple reproduction with all the available surplus above subsistence going to the state. Because the peasants had insufficient money to buy handicraft and industrial goods from the towns, the urban economies of the region were stunted and an urban bourgeoisie failed to grow. The conditions for the development of capitalism and market integration did not exist. In a situation where they were forced to perform labour services which reduced them to near-slave status, the peasantry of Eastern Europe was now clearly in a different position from the peasantry of Western Europe. Konrad and Szelenyi, like Moore, note that 'the second serfdom' (or the period that Moore refers to as 'the re-introduction of serfdom') required strong political methods to facilitate the forced (rather than market) extraction of a surplus from agriculture.

Contrary to Wittfogel, however, Konrad and Szelenyi do not conclude from the above account that the east remained frozen in some kind of 'oriental despotism'. The 'second serfdom' was to usher in a form of redistributive integration which was quite capable to sustaining economic growth. Indeed, the economy had to grow if the east were to be able to develop military strength sufficient to prevent invasion by the stronger west. Even as early as the reign of Ivan the Terrible, military industries were constructed with serf labour and, from the time of Peter the Great, western techniques of industrial organisation were employed widely by the state. As Konrad and Szelenyi and Moore see it, this was a reversal of the western pattern. In the east the nation state emerged before the nation; it was a creation of strong central governments. This was what Moore, following Lenin, called the 'Prussian' pattern of modernisation which differed from the old 'Asiatic' forms by its capacity for economic growth. Yet it was quite clear that economic security could not be guaranteed by a direct prebendal system. Consequently, a form of hereditary aristocracy was re-established, provided that it continued to serve the central state; a compromise was reached between the principles of patrimonialism and prebendalism which was to secure the compliance of the aristocracy in the process of modernisation. But the relative freedom of the aristocracy was not paralleled by the development of a bourgeoisie. Urban development remained stunted and the peasants remained as serfs.

The virtual non-existence of a bourgeoisie deprived those intellectuals, who had been influenced by western ideas, of a class with which to ally. The minor intellectual nobility, which pressed for a more rational redistributive system, was never to achieve any power in its own right. What little success it achieved, in bringing about the end of serfdom, created an economic situation which deprived it of the independent means with which to criticise the system. By the end of the nineteenth century large numbers of this stratum were forced to seek the only kind of employment open to them within the government service. Perhaps, by then, an alternative existed in alliance with a small bourgeoisie, but since a disproportionate number of that new class were Jews and other non Great Russians, racism inhibited that possibility. The fate of the intelligentsia, therefore, was closely bound up with that of the state. There was no basic conflict of interest between Church and civil bureaucracy and their two hierarchies merged to a degree unparalleled in the contemporary west. Even the police force was dominated by intellectuals and shared a common mode of discourse with its principal victims - the dissident intellectuals.

Konrad and Szelenyi depict an early twentieth century eastern route to modernisation characterised by a triple form of rule - intelligentsia, the landed interests and that prerequisite of modernisation - the barons of finance capital (who mobilised the necessary funds). There was also a sizeable body of intellectual dissent which was as impotent politically as it was significant culturally. In as much as those dissidents emulated the west in pressing for the development of market capitalism, they doomed themselves to perpetual impotence. To be sure, some reforms were undertaken to develop market relations to increase productivity and thus help bolster up royal authority but they did not result in any major accretion of power for the dissident groups. The answer seemed clear. Success for dissident groups would lie not in bourgeois reforms but in the universal application of the redistributive system. There were only two effective choices. On the one hand the reform intellectuals could enter the state administration and campaign for the triumph of the bureaucratic intelligentsia over the other two members of the triple alliance - landed interests and finance capital; or they could become professional revolutionaries and seek to destroy the land-owning classes and finance capital and perfect the bureaucratic redistributive apparatus. Konrad and Szelenyi argue that the first route was to culminate in fascism and the second route in the Bolshevik revolution. Again a dichotomous route of modernisation has been implied - the western route characterised by the growth of a strong bourgeoisie and the eastern route, with its blocked development of bourgeois power, which could result in one of two possibilities - 'socialism' or facism.

Konrad and Szelenyi portray fascism not as a temporary aberration but as a principle for making a redistributive system more rational which still finds many a receptive ear within developing economies. For redistributive sytems that have achieved a degree of modernisation, this and Bolshevism are the only routes. The end is not the ossified backward society portrayed by Wittfogel, but a more rational system capable of sustained economic growth. The systems are repressive and dictatorial but they are quite modern. They are epitomised in the contemporary Soviet and Eastern European regimes where the intelligentsia have ceased to be merely a stratum and are becoming a class which controls not only the redistributive system but also the telos - the legitimising principle.

For Konrad and Szelenyi the eastern route to modernisation involves the same kind of cultural revolution that occurred in the west - the triumph of rational organisation. It differs from the west, however, in the achievement of class power by an ascending intelligentsia capable of superceding landed interests and finance capital. The fact that working class and socialist symbols are used in its assumption of power only masks the fact that what has developed is intellectual power: it is the intellectuals who are on the road to class power. What then are the implications for revolution in the narrowly political sense? It would seem that the violent overthrow of the regime during the early stages of rational redistribution was precluded by the failure of the reform intellectuals to achieve an alliance with a bourgeoisie or its equivalent. At a later stage, however, a violent revolution became possible but not inevitable. The Bolshevik route was, indeed, highly revolutionary but Konrad and Szelenyi imply that the fascist route could have been an alternative. Whether one considers that route as necessitating the overthrow of a regime by collective violence is an open question. Hitler achieved power relatively peacefully; it was regimes in other countries which he overthrew violently.

As with Moore, the Konrad and Szelenyi thesis, though stimulating, raises profound questions both of theory and with regard to evidence. One wonders how it is theoretically possible for a class to be constituted by a principle of legitimation. One wonders also whether the category 'intellectuals' is discrete enough. In contemporary 'socialist' societies, there seems to be a constant cleavage between established Party bureaucrats, technical management, and humanist intellectuals: this might suggest that each group operates with a different conception of the telos. One suspects also that the 'fascist' route has been misrepresented. For us, fascism differs from other right wing authoritarian regimes by the capacity of its elite to mobilise a high degree of popular support. It is essentially the product of a society where mass communications have developed and industrialisation is well under way. Significantly the major support for Hitler came not from East Prussia but from the industrialised west and south (which were always outside the redistributive system). Mussolini also drew major support from industrialised North Italy rather than the south which was going through the very early stages of rational modernisation. What would qualify as fascist regimes under the Konrad and Szelenyi formula are countries like Horthy's Hungary or perhaps Spain under Franco. Both regimes were highly authoritarian but both imported fascist ideology from elsewhere. In neither of them did the intelligentsia make any inroads against landed interests and finance capital. Indeed the opposite was the case.

In terms of the use of evidence, one suspects that Konrad and Szelenyi make too much of the continued role of a prebendal system in nineteenth century Russia. They underrate the extent to which a Russian bourgeoisie had developed with very strong western connections. Indeed the international role of capitalism does not feature as a major explanatory element. Finally, though we would agree that the Soviet Union and Eastern Europe are, in fact, divided into classes and that the working class does not rule, recent events in Poland leave no doubt that the working class is more politically significant than is claimed in either the Moore or the Konrad and Szelenyi theses.

The Objective Idealist View

In the picture of modernisation, outlined by Konrad and Szelenyi, there is clearly an element of what we have referred to as 'objective idealism'. However critical those authors might be of Hegel, there is a sense where they portray the Hegelian ideal of rationality working itself out. Indeed such a view is difficult to avoid.

The Hegelian view·was both a product of and a reaction to the eighteenth century Enlightenment. That Enlightenment combined two very different views about the relationship of human beings to history. On the one hand, there was the liberal view that human beings made their own history and that a new rational order might be constructed by humans, for humans, on human principles. It was this belief that promoted the French revolutionaries to reorganise the calendar beginning with a new year one, and to invent new weights and measures. It was a similar view which led the American revolutionaries to design a new constitution to herald 'the new beginning'.[32] On the other hand, the Enlightenment tended to raise the concept 'Reason' to a metaphysical principle. It was as if human action was the product of Reason rather than the opposite. Is there little wonder then that the cult of Reason became an object of worship in no less a place than the cathedral of Notre Dame?

The contribution of Hegel, as has been noted, was to locate the development of Reason in the unfolding of the universal Mind towards greater freedom. It was such a view which saw the aftermath of the French Revolution in terms of the spirit of a new age (or as Hegel would put it the latest manifestation of the universal Mind). There was a need, therefore, to examine the essential features of this new spirit and contrast it with the spirit of preceding ages. This was the task undertaken by Henri de Rouvroy, Comte de Saint-Simon the founder of modern theories of 'industrialism'.[33] In Saint-Simon's interpretation, human life passed through three major creative ages. The first of these was classical antiquity. The second was mediaeval Christendom and the third was the age of science and industry. Each of these ages was preceded by a destructive phase, the last of which had been heralded by the Enlightenment and carried on by the French Revolution. The slate was now clean for the rule of the rational and productive classes - les industriels (capitalists plus workers) who would displace les oisifs (the landowners and idle remnants of the past). The dynamic of this whole process, it seems, was not so much the clash of material interests but the unfolding of some equivalent of the Hegelian universal Mind which had found its apogee in Saint-Simon's new science-based religion.

For Saint-Simon, revolution was not so much a part of the process of modernisation as its precursor. The ideas of les industriels would now spread out over the whole world and people would realise their self-evident superiority. But would they? If there was one thing which the French Revolution had shown, it was Marx's dictum that although human beings made their own history it was not always in the way they intended. Burke would surely have agreed with such a statement and so indeed would most of the founding fathers of the discipline which came to be known as 'sociology'.

It is fashionable nowadays to follow the French sociologist Raymond Aron in tracing the origins of sociology back to the Enlightenment and specifically to the liberal writings of Montesquieu.[34] In fact, sociology was not so much the product of the Enlightenment but of the failure of its voluntaristic hopes. There is, after all, an unbridgeable chasm between the basic premise of classical liberalism - the pre-social individual with self-evident human rights and that of sociology - the determined individual whose rights are historical conventions. There have, of course,

---

32. H. Arendt, On Revolution (1963), Penguin, Harmondsworth, 1973, pp. 28-9.

33. A good anthology of Saint-Simon's works in K. Taylor (ed.), Henri Saint-Simon, 1760-1825, Selected Writings on Science, Industry and Social Organisation, Croom Helm, London, 1975.

34. See R. Aron, Main Currents in Sociological Thought, Vol. 1, Penguin, Harmondsworth, 1968, p. 17.

been many noble attempts to bridge the gap and it is no accident that the most famous and most convincing of all the liberals - John Stuart Mill - spent much of his life in such an exercise. But the gap still remains.

The source of Mill's liberalism was his father James Mill and the most famous of all the utilitarians - Jeremy Bentham. The source of Mill's sociological views, however, was the one time secretary of Saint-Simon, Auguste Comte, the person who coined the term 'sociology' in the first place. Following Saint-Simon, Comte once again divided human history into three epochs[35] traversed by some equivalent of the universal Mind. The first of these - the theological epoch - was characterised by humans explaining nature in terms of forces, such as gods and spirits, which were similar to humans themselves. The second - the metaphysical - occurred when humans sought explanations in abstractions such as natural law. The third epoch, ushered in by the French Revolution, was the age of positivism which demanded an observation of the external world and a discovery of its laws. Since in principle these laws were no different from the laws of physics and mathematics, the goal was a unified science which would inform a restructured efficient social order. In such a view there should be no place for revolution. Even the Great French Revolution had resulted in the rule of Napoleon I, a manifestation of the reversion to the old theological and military age. But at least that revolution had cleared some of the dead wood away and so indeed had the French Revolution of 1848. This time, however, it had resulted in the rule of Napoleon III, who promised an end to 'feudal' monarchy, an end to outdated English parliamentarianism and the establishment of a managerial state which enshrined the Comtean ideas of 'order and progress'. So long as progress was equated with order, revolutions could only be justified in terms of re-establishing order. Significantly the Brazilian 'revolution' of 1964, which flew the national flag emblazoned with the Comtean slogan 'order and progress' was justified in terms of a Comtean view of 'order'. The subsequent 'Brazilian miracle' of economic development has been pursued by means of vicious policies which would make the rule of Napoleon III seem almost benign.

Managerialist ideas, such as those of Saint-Simon and Comte were to remain influential throughout most of the nineteenth century, though the rejection of <u>laissez faire</u> capitalism by the early sociologists[36] gave way to the exaltation of a self-regulating economic system which seemed to be bringing about general abundance. In the heartlands of capitalism, the attention of scholars shifted from an explanation of the dynamics of change to an examination of the working of 'iron laws of economics' valid for all time. These 'iron laws' were based on the utilitarian view of human beings as unchanging psychological types pursuing pleasure and avoiding pain. With such a view one could only explain progress in terms of a reified conception of 'technology'. We shall return to the question of technological

---

35. A. Comte, <u>Cours de Philosophie Positive</u>, Vol. I, 1st lecture (1829) in S. Andreski (ed.), <u>The Essential Comte</u>, Croom Helm, London, 1974, pp. 19-41.

36. A. Comte, <u>System of Positive Polity or Treatise on Sociology, Instituting the Religion of Humanity</u> (1851-54), Burt Franklin, New York, reprint of 1875 edn., Vol. I, p. 124.

determinism in the next section. In the meantime let us note that the explanation of progress in the wider sense of the word was left to the discipline of sociology which began by deriving much inspiration from biological theories of evolution.

It is easy to see why sociologists were unsatisfied with the mechanical metaphor used widely by economists. After all machines do not evolve. Biological organisms most certainly do and it was biological analogy which was to inform the most famous of the nineteenth century British sociologists - Herbert Spencer.[37] As Spencer saw it, progress consisted in greater complexity of organisation, more and more elaborate division of labour and an increase in the size of society. Nowadays our knowledge of mediaeval history and social anthropology is such that Spencer's views seem very naive. What has changed over the past few hundred years is not the scope of the complexity of the division of labour but the nature of the specialised tasks performed. But that is by the way. What is important to the argument here is that biological analogy tends to be used by critics of revolution. Revolution is aberrant!

As adherents to biological metaphor saw them revolutions impeded modernisation. Evolution, on the other hand, was the very stuff of modernisation. At least this was the case after Darwin's <u>Origin of Species</u> appeared in 1859. Inevitably the use of biological analogy in the social sciences was to result in a number of forms of 'Social Darwinism'. Those societies which survived were those which were best able to adapt to their environment. At one extreme, Social Darwinism took on overtly racist tones and the 'survival of the fittest' was interpreted as the 'survival of the strongest'; such views were to become very influential amongst Nazi social scientists in the twentieth century. The Nazi revolution, as they saw it, was less a manifestation of the universal Mind (<u>Zeitgeist</u>) than the triumph of the national spirit (<u>Volksgeist</u>) of the 'most fit' people; the universal would result from the domination of the particular. At the other extreme, Social Darwinism was interpreted to serve anarchist ends. Kropotkin, in his <u>Mutual Aid</u>,[38] for example, saw the 'survival of the fittest' as the survival of those most able to co-operate. Everywhere the spirit of co-operation was growing in the womb of capitalist society and the national states were becoming obsolescent. Thus, for Kropotkin, modernisation consisted in a kind of <u>cultural</u> revolution. This required adaptation to a world which required more and more co-operation. Kropotkin's equivalent of the universal Mind, it would seem, was capable of making that adaptation peacefully. Though revolutions in the narrowly political sense of overthrowing a regime by collective violence were likely, they were by no means inevitable.

In discussing anarchism, we have come a long way from Hegel's view of the universal Mind. For Hegel, one realisation of the universal Mind was the development of the universal rational 'class' - the bureaucracy. Hegel, therefore, came to admire the Prussian state whereas the anarchists sought to destroy it. Indeed this was the pre-requisite for the attainment of

---

37.   H. Spencer, <u>The Study of Sociology</u>, Uni. of Michigan Press, Ann Arbor, 1961, especially pp. 298-323.

38.   P. Kropotkin, <u>Mutual Aid: A Factor in Evolution</u> (1902 revised in 1904 and 1914), Allen Lane, London, 1972.

Reason and the overcoming of alienation. The anarchists came in all shapes and sizes but all agreed on the need for a cultural revolution and for most of them this was premised on some kind of natural law and the realisation of some equivalent of the universal Mind. For all his professed materialism, this was the position taken by perhaps the most famous of the anarchists, Michael Bakunin. Bakunin, however, differed most radically from Kropotkin in tracing the relationship between the necessary cultural revolution and revolution in the sense of the overthrow of regimes by collective violence.[39] For Bakunin these were inseparable since the most downtrodden sections of society (called by Marx the lumpenproletariat) had to acquire the self-confidence necessary to recover their humanity by engaging in collective violence. This theme was to be frequently reiterated in the twentieth century and finds its most blatant contemporary expression in the writings of the one-time psychologist Frantz Fanon. The road to liberation is through violence.[40]

There is insufficient space here for us to discuss the manifestation of 'objective idealism' amongst liberals and Christian theorists in the late nineteenth century. We excuse ourselves on the grounds that such writers usually had little to say about revolution. Suffice it to note that by the time of the First World War the objective idealist strand in social thought had suffered a marked decline. Indeed that war had given rise to very serious doubts about the notion of progress. Whilst many Marxists celebrated the Russian October Revolution, the general mood amongst non-Marxist social scientists was explicitly counter-revolutionary. But it was a counter-revolutionary mood very different from that which had pertained amongst organicist social scientists in the nineteenth century. Many of the earlier generation of social scientists, whilst criticising revolution in their own era, were not wholly dismissive of the great French Revolution ushered in in 1789. In the 1920s the tendency was to equate the Great French Revolution with the Bolshevik Revolution and uniformly to condemn both.

A classic work of the period was Pitirim Sorokin's The Sociology of Revolution (1925)[41] which portrayed revolution as a disease affecting the body politic and its constituent parts which succumbed eventually to a Thermidor (a return to normality). Revolutions, of which the latest and most insidious was that of the Bolsheviks, never contributed anything of worth to humanity since nothing of value remained which could compensate for the destruction which revolutions caused. Sorokin's work was to give rise to a considerable body of literature which elaborated the disease model

---

39.   Bakunin's phrase 'the passion for destruction is a creative passion' has been much quoted; 'The Revolution in Germany' (1842), in S. Dolgoff (ed.), Bakunin on Anarchy: Selected Works by the Activist-Founder of World Anarchism, George Allen and Unwin, London, 1973, p. 57. For an example of Bakunin's more developed position see, 'The Program of the International Brotherhood' (1869), in ibid., pp. 149-55.

40.   F. Fanon, The Wretched of the Earth, Penguin, Harmondsworth, 1967.

41.   P. Sorokin, The Sociology of Revolution, Howard Fertig, New York, 1967.

26.

and was to culminate in Crane Brinton's The Anatomy of Revolution (1938) which traced the process of revolution from infection through fever to the recovery of normality.[42] The persistent and universal call was for experts on counter-revolution who were some species of epidemiologist.

Though Sorokin was disillusioned with the idea of progress, it is clear from his larger and much more famous work Social and Cultural Dynamics (1937)[43] that he had not forsaken the objective idealist position. In this work, Sorokin depicted not a linear nor spiral development of the universal Mind but its manifestation in the form of fluctuation between Ideational (ideological or spiritual) cultures and Sensate (materialistic) cultures. What his contemporaries called 'progress' was merely a set of outcomes stemming from their Sensate (materialist) view of the world. In the eleventh century or perhaps in two or three centuries hence, people's idea of progress was and will be very different.

Sorokin's 1937 work is relevant to the study of revolution in that he attempted to correlate the degree of social turbulence in Europe with the rise and fall of the different types of culture. His study went back to Ancient Greece though his main focus was on the period 500 AD to 1933. He concluded that significant social disturbances were extremely frequent throughout the whole period, the span of time between such disturbances ranging from 8.6 years (Byzantium, 532-1390) to 2.4 years (Spain, 467-1933). Since such was the case there was no major European nation which was inherently disorderly or inherently orderly. In general most of the internal crises in the life processes of these 'social bodies' were, like the crises in the life process of the individual, only of a few weeks duration. The magnitude of the disturbances did not, it appears, fluctuate very much over time and there was no definite trend towards greater order or greater disorder. Nevertheless, three periods did stand out as being more disorderly than others. These were the 8th century, the 13th-14th century and the 19th-20th century. The first of these saw significant changes in the dominant Ideational Culture which gave rise to what the sociologist Emile Durkheim called widespread anomie (the loss of social bearings and a decline in confidence in social norms). The second, the 13th-14th century, was a major period of transition between Ideational and Sensate Culture which had the same social effect. Finally the 19th century, ushered in by the Great French Revolution, saw the liquidation of the last vestiges of Ideational Culture; this produced initial turmoil followed by relative calm (the last quarter of the 19th century) and renewed disorder as the dominant Sensate Culture began to break down. We are led, therefore, to expect not greater peace but an increase in disorder as a new Ideational Culture takes shape.

Clearly the change between cultures is what we have referred to earlier as 'cultural' revolutions and a convincing case might be made for Sorokin's periodisation. One wonders, however, why the 8th century was so significant and whether the 15th-17th centuries were not more important in terms of cultural change. As for the 20th century, we shall go on to argue

---

42.   C. Brinton, The Anatomy of Revolution (1938) revised and
        expanded edition, Vintage Books, New York, 1965.

43.   P. Sorokin, Social and Cultural Dynamics, Bedminster Press,
        New York, 1962 - the following is taken from Vol. III,   pp. 383-506.

that there are few signs as yet (and fewer in the period 1900-33) that the dominant Sensate culture is breaking down. Our major methodological argument with Sorokin, however, centres on the concept of 'revolution' in the sense of the overthrow of a regime by collective violence. The use of this term is perhaps only meaningful in considering the past three centuries and Sorokin's aggregate data (albeit broken down into types of disturbance) does not help us make many useful conclusions.

Despite the criticisms, Sorokin's 1937 study will be of value when we come to the next chapter where we look at studies of the contemporary third world. His longitudinal focus serves as a healthy corrective for those who see the prospect of revolution or violence receding as countries become more like us (or the Soviet Union). His assertion that there is not a strong correlation between the rapidity of change and the degree of violence openly challenges much contemporary literature. Finally his thesis that the really significant correlation is between violence and the clash of cultures with different notions of modernisation should be required reading for all those who were surprised by the recent events in Iran.

Sorokin's Social and Cultural Dynamics was published just before the Second World War. With the revival of the social sciences in the Long Boom which followed that war, people tended to remember Sorokin not for his anticipation of violence and revolution as Sensate culture declined but for his earlier and most violent attacks on the Bolshevik Revolution. Here his objective idealism was less obvious and his 1925 study was more in tune with that very ideological mood known as 'the end of ideology'. In recent years, however, there has been something of a rebirth of the objective idealist position. Most significant has been the revival of Marxism in a Hegelian form. There has also been the spectacular rise of liberation theology which at times has attempted to reconcile Hegelian Marxism with a Christian Zeitgeist and to pursue a programme which is most revolutionary. There have, moreover, been attempts once again to reconcile the themes of evolution and revolution. A notable example here is the work of the sociologist W.F. Wertheim.[44]

In contrast to some of the theorists discussed earlier in this section, who are 'objective idealists' only implicitly, Wertheim is a self-confessed one. In his view, evolution is governed by a principle of emancipation which comes more and more to realise itself. In his own words he is a finalist - an approach which we have defined earlier as teleological. This is the formulation of a process according to where it will lead to, as opposed to determinism - the formulation of a process according to where it starts. This teleological view and a claim to be able to predict future events Wertheim attempts to reconcile with voluntarism - the belief in free will.

It is not at all clear whether Wertheim's attempted reconciliation succeeds; nevertheless his description of the emancipation principle is extremely stimulating. Human history, he claims, is proceeding from the emancipation of humankind from nature to emancipation from other human beings. In this process, revolution is no more than accelerated evolution and counter-revolution is simply a decline in the opportunities for emancipation. To this schema is added the concept, borrowed from Clifford Geertz, of 'involution' which signifies a process of emancipation

---

44. Wertheim, op.cit.

which will lead to a dead end. Thus the events in France after 1789 were indeed a revolution, not just in the sense of the overthrow of a regime by collective violence but in Wertheim's sense of contributing towards the emancipation of the French people. What happened after 1933 in Germany was a counter-revolution in that the opportunities for emancipation declined. Finally the Indonesian developments are seen as 'involutionary' because they are leading to a dead end.

The problem with the above typology is that we are never quite sure whether what is claimed to be a revolution actually furthers the cause of human emancipation until long after the event. Just how do we know that involution has taken place until the dead end is reached? What do we do with the Bolshevik Revolution which, according to Wertheim, was followed by a 'Thermidor' (a shift to more conservative policies and values)? For Wertheim, the Soviet people are much more emancipated now than in 1917; thus the Bolshevik Revolution was indeed a contributor to emancipation. But suppose that regime becomes more and more repressive, does that alter the status of what happened in 1917 or do we decide long after the event that a counter-revolution has occurred? Who can say, moreover, just what the status of the Iranian revolution might be at the present? In making his concept of emancipation twofold - emancipation from the forces of nature, and emancipation from domination by privileged individuals, Wertheim has charted a course that leaves him with a dilemma. If emancipation and its attendant human progress is to be from the forces of nature, then the most efficient development of the productive process can be equated with human progress. At the same time Wertheim, following Arendt, places equal emphasis upon co-operation and emancipation from domination.

The tension between these two concepts becomes evident when Wertheim attempts to discuss the events of Hungary in 1956. In the light of his notions of revolution and counter-revolution it is not surprising that for Wertheim the events in Hungary in 1956 are best described as 'ambiguous'. From the position of his twofold notion of emancipation he must argue that if Premier Nagy's movement was an attempt efficiently to develop the productive forces, in terms of emancipation from the forces of nature it was progressive and thus revolutionary. On the other hand, Nagy's movement had as a part of its platform the reversal of rural collect-ivisation with an attendant decrease in human co-operation. Such a programme can be seen as counter-revolutionary. Even with the benefit of the hindsight necessary for assessing revolution in Wertheim's terms, it is extremely difficult to assess the general tendency of revolutions (or counter-revolutions) which cross Wertheim's twofold categorisation of emancipation. This difficulty is not helped at all by the fact that, though the Hungarian uprising was abortive in terms of its stated immediate aims, events in Hungary in 1956 can be seen to have contributed to the subsequent adoption of policies for economic reform. These on the one hand have promoted the development of the productive forces, and on the other have decreased co-operative human action in the work place by stressing competition between industrial enterprises and between individual workers.

The picture becomes even more complicated when we consider Wertheim's view that progress is not linear but occurs in dialectical leaps with 'the poor and blank' (a term borrowed from Mao Zedong) leaping ahead of the most advanced. This is supported by the arguments of people such as Romein (who talks about the 'law of the retarding lead'), Service (who talks in terms of a 'leapfrog effect'), Sahlins' point that backward feudalism had the potential to leap ahead of the more advanced Roman Empire, and similar arguments deriving from Engels, Lenin, Trotsky and, of course, Mao Zedong. But what are the conditions under which a backward country leaps ahead? It is never, according to Wertheim, the most backward country which does so. How then do we spot the potential front runner?

The notion of 'leap-frog' is beset with enormous problems for the social scientist. Nevertheless, as a description of what happened to certain societies in the course of their revolutions, it does have much empirical validity. The problem is how to move from a description of particular histories to a social science generalisation.

More fruitful, perhaps, for the social scientist, is Wertheim's discussion of 'counterpoint values'. Wertheim maintains that every dominant value system in a society depends for its success on the point to which it can incorporate counterpoint values. An example here will help. The legitimisation of papal hierarchy in the Roman Catholic Church depends for its success upon the incorporation into its legitimising ideology of the notion that the rich person can as easily enter the Kingdom of God as the camel pass through the eye of a needle. The domination of a bourgeois elite in liberal society, moreover, depends upon the incorporation of the idea of equality before the law. It is wrong, therefore, to see society always in terms of competing value systems. Rather one should look at the institutionalisation of counterpoints. Once that institutionalisation breaks down, there are preconditions for revolution. Finally, revolution consists in the situation where the deinstitutionalised subordinate values become the new dominant values.

What are the preconditions which make for the deinstitutionalisation of counterpoint values? Here Wertheim distinguishes between two types of revolution. The bourgeois revolution in the West comes about when economic growth and increasing vertical mobility is met by an intransigent elite and occurs always in an authoritarian system. Peasant revolutions, however, occur in conditions of extreme poverty, where there is a lack of opportunity for vertical social mobility for the masses but considerable horizontal mobility (between regions and between jobs) and finally where there is a harsh political system. This latter set of conditions, however, needs to be activated by what he calls an accelerator. This term, borrowed from the political scientist Chalmers Johnson,[45] signifies a set of features which become important only when the basic preconditions are present. They may include a crisis in government finances, a lost or losing war etc. But the problem remains in deciding whether or not those accelerators are in fact basic preconditions.

The presence of the preconditions for peasant revolution in many countries today suggests that Wertheim sees revolution as a basic feature of modernisation (which must involve emancipation). He believes, moreover, that these revolutions will take the political form of the overthrow of a regime by collective violence. The two cases of non-violent revolution which he cites, India and the Chinese Cultural Revolution (which were both apparently revolutions from below led from above), only qualify as non-violent by a considerable stretch of the imagination.

---

45. C. Johnson, Revolutionary Change, University of London Press, London, 1968, pp. 91, 99-100, 103-105, 153-54.

Let us now summarise the objective idealist position. The view that progress might be reduced to a single principle has been embraced by both supporters of revolution and their opponents. For Saint-Simon and Comte, the only place for revolution was in the past. For Kropotkin the realisation of the emancipatory principle based on co-operative adaptation did not require collective violence though that was the usual outcome. A similar position is taken by Wertheim, for whom revolution is simply the acceleration of evolution. In contrast were those who, following Bakunin, saw collective violence as necessary to the emancipation of the human spirit. Finally came those who, like Sorokin, saw collective violence as a normal characteristic of human history (albeit an abhorrent one) which would intensify at times of inevitable cultural revolution.

Technological Determinism

At first sight technological determinism appears to be theoretically impossible. After all technology can be no more than the way human beings organise themselves and elements of the natural world in order to pursue goals independent of technology. According to the Greek tradition, technology falls into the category techne (means) which only have significance in relation to some end (telos). This point was clearly perceived by the founders of the ideology of industrialism - Saint Simon and Comte - who, for all their 'scientism', had ultimate recourse to an objective idealist theory of progress. Marx also, whilst praising the capitalist mode of production for its unprecedented development of technology, did not see technology alone as accounting for the change in modes of production. His focus was rather on the contradiction between the relations of production and the forces of production and these latter included human organisation itself. That human organisation presupposed historically-determined ends and, indeed, the communist future was predicated upon human beings recovering themselves from alienation and developing their potentiality to produce co-operatively. There was, therefore, in Marx an implicit telos. The social Darwinists, from fascists to anarchists, moreover, did not see human societies passively adapting themselves to an external environment, since in the process of adaptation the human environment was also changed according to ends determined by humans themselves. How then is technological determinism possible?

In our opinion arguments based on technological determinism are, in fact, theoretically incoherent though, in practice, they inform the overwhelming bulk of social thought in east and west. In the west, according to the philosopher Jacques Ellul, the technological means chosen to achieve ends formulated in the past have been elevated to such a position that the original ends have often been forgotten.[46] In the contemporary world, human ends tend to be expressed simply as an ensemble of techniques designed originally for ends which are no longer discussed. This process may be seen most clearly in the ideology of economic growth. Not many people nowadays ask about the purposes which growth is to serve. Indeed, production is carried on to satisfy human needs which are themselves produced by the same process. In that situation human beings are reduced

---

46.   J. Ellul, The Technological Society (1954), Alfred S. Knopf, New York, 1967.

merely to recording devices for the result of techniques - a job which machines are now learning to do more efficiently. The cultural revolution of our time is one in which human beings are reduced to cogs in a machine which greater efficiency makes increasingly disposable.

In the east a similar process is under way. This has been achieved by purging Marxism of its human content and redefining Marx's forces of production in an exclusively technical sense. The relations of production are increasingly seen as merely a reflection of the stage of economic growth. A milestone in this development was the Stalin constitution of 1936 which defined socialism as a static model determined by the forces of production.[47] Yet even Stalin, for all his crudity, was to recoil at the extreme manifestation of the Soviet version of the 'logic of industrialism' and castigated the would-be textbook writer Yaroshenko for casting communism purely in terms of rational organisation.[48] Khrushchev's vision of communism, which in the early 1960s he prophesied as arriving by 1981,[49] was somewhat less arid, and yet one is still left with the view that the social and moral transformation to communism would develop automatically once the productive forces had reached a certain level. The vision of 'mature socialism'[50] provided by the present Soviet leadership is, of course, less ambitious. It is, however, more dismal and one is left simply with the vision of a technocratic future. Modernisation defined in terms of technological development has apparently become an end rather than a means. Since the dynamics of the transition to the communist 'telos' are no longer explored, there can now only be more of the same kind of growth fetishism which characterises the west.

What then are the implications for revolution? Could it be that, contrary to Sorokin, the major cultural revolution of our time consists in the revolution of 'sensate' universality where east and west converge in a world in which confused means and ends are produced by some inhuman automation? Could the ex-Trotskyist James Burnham be right in seeing the

47.   J. Stalin, 'On the Draft Constitution of the U.S.S.R.,' 25 November 1936, in J. Stalin, Problems of Leninism, op.cit., pp. 540-68. See also the discussion in B. Brugger, 'Soviet and Chinese Views on Revolution and Socialism - Some Thoughts on the Problems of Diachrony and Synchrony', Journal of Contemporary Asia, Vol. XI, No. 3, September 1981, pp. 311-32.

48.   J. Stalin, Economic Problems of Socialism in the U.S.S.R. (1952), Peking, Foreign Languages Press, 1972, p. 62.

49.   Communist Party of the Soviet Union, Programme, 31 October 1961, London, Soviet Booklet, No. 83, 1961.

50.   See A. Evans, 'Developed Socialism in Soviet Ideology', Soviet Studies Vol. XXIX, No. 3, July 1977, pp. 409-20; M. Lavigne, 'Advanced Socialist Society', Economy and Society, Vol. VII, No. 4, November 1978, pp. 367-94.

major revolution of our time as a 'managerial revolution' where a managerial class assumes the role of the proletariat in the work of Marx?[51]

In Burnham's view (written in 1941), Marx was completely correct in his portrayal of the mechanisms under which capitalism would self-destruct. His mistake, however, lay in putting faith in the proletariat. The bourgeois revolution occurred because the capitalist mode of production had developed in the womb of feudal society. But in capitalist society, socialism was not developing at all. Rather one saw the development of a new class of managers, which did not own the means of production in the bourgeois sense of legal ownership. It, in fact, was coming to own the states in which it operated and, as owner of the state, was able to promote institutions which permeated society with a new managerial ideology. The logic of industrialism and technical ideology were portrayed as universal values in the same way as the liberal notion of human rights was portrayed in the bourgeois revolution. In fact, both ideologies rationalised the interests of the new dominant class. The dictatorships which Burnham saw all around him were modern analogues of the autocratic regimes which heralded the advent of capitalism. These would eventually yield to less oppressive regimes once the position of the new class was secure.

Burnham's work, which appeared in 1941, has been widely criticised for the failure of his predictions. He prophesied the victory of the managerially-oriented Axis powers and felt that the Soviet Union would split into two parts with the Eastern and Western portions gravitating to Japan and Germany, the new super-managerial states. His portrayal of Roosevelt's New Deal as a harbinger of the end of capitalism in that country now seems rather quaint. Nevertheless, Burnham was to be the forerunner of a mass of literature on 'the new industrial state' which sees the major revolution of our time as managerial. In more recent times John Kenneth Galbraith, a liberal at heart, has observed that the only hope for liberal values lies in the autonomy of the universities in an increasingly technocratic world.[52]

In industrial countries the new technocracy, it would seem, tends to remove the notion of revolution as the overthrow of a regime by collective violence from the self-writing computer programme which has replaced history. Amongst the technocratic intelligentsia, the most one may hope for is a reconceptualisation of revolution in terms dictated by the machine itself. In such a case autonomous human action is granted only to an elite which may perform the task of systems-engineer. The task of the social scientist is to specify the functions performed by the social machine, locate the structures performing them and suggest means whereby the elite may prevent disfunctions and systems breakdown. With such a view it is easy to see why revolution (system breakdown) was seen merely as an extreme manifestation of violence in general (system strain).

The above structural-functionalist view was to inform two very influential books on revolution which appeared in the mid-1960s. These were Chalmers Johnson's <u>Revolution and the Social System</u> (1964) and

---

51.   Burnham, <u>op.cit.</u>

52.   J. Galbraith, <u>The New Industrial State</u>, 2nd revised edn., Houghton Mifflin, Boston, 1971, pp. 382-83.

Revolutionary Change (1966).[53]   Briefly, and we excuse the jargon, revolutions are caused by a disequilibrated social system where society's values and ways of adapting to the external environment change in a way such that necessary social functions may no longer be performed. A disequilibrated social system is one which has experienced 'multiple disfunctions'. These include a failure in socialisation (the way values are transmitted), disagreement over basic social goals and a lack of synchronisation of social roles.   Such multiple disfunctions may be internally generated due to environmental change or the rise of new ideologies or externally generated due to war, imports of technology etc.   The key variable, however, is not the number and scope of the multiple disfunctions but the response of the governing elite.   A revolution will occur when a governing elite fails to remedy the situation and loses legitimacy. It may try to compensate for this legitimation crisis by coercive measures but it might also lose control over the instruments of coercion.   In short revolutions are cases of failed systems management.

Stripped to its bare essentials, Johnson's account is not a theory of revolution at all.   It is an elaborate, and at times highly sophisticated, taxonomy of factors one needs to take into account if one is to explain revolution, assuming of course that the basic axiom about social functions holds.   Such a taxonomy could only become a theory if one was told what determines the successful or unsuccessful response of the governing elite. Alas, all we have is a blueprint for the social machine and the hope that the engineer will be intelligent enough to know how to operate it.   Presumably the modernisation which engenders multiple disfunctions also improves the ability of an elite to overcome them.   The trouble arises when one considers that the engineer is, in fact, part of the blueprint.

Only a few years after the publication of Johnson's books, the secure prospect of a programmed future came increasingly to be rejected in the industrialised countries.   The youth explosions of the late 1960s were symptomatic of the reaction. A major influence here was the philosopher Herbert Marcuse[54] who saw all around him a society more 'totalitarian' than anything produced in the Soviet Union.   The Soviet Union was still in the relatively inefficient stage of repression and had yet to reach the ultimate technique of control - repressive tolerance.   His solution lay in the disorganised revolt of marginal people whose assimilation into the new totalitarian society has been less thorough.   Though Marcuse himself was not an apostle of violence, one cannot but note that the appeal to marginal groups would yield eventually to an affirmation of the creative role of violence in the manner of Bakunin and Frantz Fanon.

Since the late 1960s, Marcuse's prospect of a revolution of marginal people has receded.   In this age of economic crises and neutron bombs, there has developed a mood of dispirited resignation and a lack of hope in

---

53.   C. Johnson, Revolution and the Social System, Stanford University Press, 1964 and C. Johnson, Revolutionary Change, op.cit.

54.   H. Marcuse, One Dimensional Man: The Ideology of Industrial Society, Sphere Books, London, 1968;   H. Marcuse, 'Repressive Tolerance', in R. Wolff, B. Moore Jr. and H. Marcuse, A Critique of Pure Tolerance, Jonathan Cape, London, 1969, pp. 95-137.

any revolutionary change. But are Burnham and Galbraith right in that the final revolution has already taken place and a technocratic class is already in power? Perhaps Marcuse's 'totalitarian society' is irremovable, though clearly it is now much less comfortable. Surely such a conclusion would constitute a denial of history. There are always contradictory trends in every society and these apply as much to any intellectual elite as to any other group in society.

Such, indeed is the argument of the late Alvin Gouldner in his work, The Future of Intellectuals and the Rise of the New Class.[55] For Gouldner, Galbraith's assertion that a technological elite is already dominant was 'superficial'. The technological elite has not yet been institutionalised, neither is there any functional necessity for its existence. Nevertheless it would be naive to claim, in the manner of Noam Chomsky, that the growing technological elite is subservient to the old monied elites.[56] On the contrary there is a growing tension between the two elites and, of the two, it is clearly the former which is developing into a new class.

The position of Gouldner is at the same time more extravagant and more cautious than that adopted by Konrad and Szelenyi. It is more extravagant in that Gouldner claims that the new intellectual class is not just a product of a particular society but is <u>universal</u>. It is more cautious, however, in that its internal contradictions (technocracy versus humanism) render it forever flawed. This flaw is reflected in the very rationality it claims for itself. That rationality is much wider than one which derives solely from technological efficiency. Whilst clearly the new class is born of and possesses the scientific knowledge and technical skills on which the future development of the productive forces depend, it has at the same time no wish to develop the forces of production solely for the sake of profit. Its very claim to superiority over the old monied classes rests not only on the latter's lack of technical credentials but also to the 'taint' of profit and lack of concern for society at large. The claim of the new class to represent society at large, however, is partially belied by the use to which it puts its 'cultural capital' which can only increase its own share or the national product and reproduce the social conditions for its ever increasing appropriation. This flaw is, indeed, no different from that of the old monied class.

How then may the new class overcome its fatal flaw? At first the going is easy because it can divert hostility on to the remnants of the old monied class. Eventually, however, it must press into service its humanistic wing to rationalise its anti-egalitarianism and celebrate its technological mission. But how willing is that wing to provide what Wertheim would have called the counterpoint which serves to institutionalise the dominant values? How willing is the humanistic wing to promote values such as workers' control whilst cementing the conditions under which such control becomes impossible? How effectively may one separate the efforts of the humanistic wing to promote critical discourse at the level of theory whilst the technocratic wing rewards its clients for

---

55. A. Gouldner, The Future of Intellectuals and the Rise of the New Class, Macmillan Press, London, 1979.

56. N. Chomsky, American Power and the New Mandarins, Penguin, Harmondsworth, 1969.

their conformity to expectations fostered by indoctrination? How does one reconcile the humanistic concern that practice be consistent with theory with the technocratic claim that practice is legitimate only if it is seen to conform to a reasonable rule? At the root of all these contradictions is the conflict between the technocratic view that domination is the road to truth and the humanistic obligation to examine all prevailing assumptions. Before long the 'anti-present', which Wertheim would have called the counterpoint of the 'present', will surely become deinstitutionalised. Or if one prefers Gouldner's formulation 'the culture of critical discourse must put its hands round its own throat and see how long it can squeeze'. Though the new class is on the ascendant, its internal contradictions offer the vista of future revolutionary change.[57]

The most obvious criticism of the Gouldner thesis is the extravagance of its claims. After all that has been said in this chapter about multilinear routes to modernisation, it is difficult at this point to argue that history has fundamentally changed and what is now emerging is a universal techno-logical class. Whilst Gouldner does not wish to imply a general convergence theory, it is clear that this is what he does. Moreover, though Gouldner claims that he is in the Hegelian objective idealist tradition, there is always the underlying determinist assumption that society merely adapts itself to an external technological environment. This is a long way from the point with which we began this chapter - the Hegelian mission of locating the development of Reason in the unfolding of the universal Mind towards greater freedom.

Conclusion

This chapter has examined four ways of looking at how the 'advanced industrial societies' have got to be the way that they are. Within each there have been theorists who have asserted the need for revolution (approvingly or otherwise) and those who have denied it. The easiest definition to deal with is the cultural one. Most people nowadays would define modernisation itself as a type of cultural revolution though one still finds echoes of the view, prevalent in Japan and China in the late nineteenth century, that the essence of a national culture might be retained whilst foreign industrial techniques are imported from the west. This was the view which informed Japan's Meiji restoration which Moore considered to be a kind of revolution. Such a view seems very old fashioned nowadays but the recent Islamic revolution in Iran would suggest that it is often disregarded at a regime's peril.

There is also probably little disagreement that some kind of revolution in the political economy sense of the word is necessary to modernisation. But even here there are people who consider the industrial revolution to have been a mistake and to have led inevitably to the society described by Ellul or Marcuse. Major disagreement on this score tends to arise when one considers the types of political economic revolution necessary in the past and those which might be necessary in the future. An orthodox Stalinist would assert the need for both a bourgeois revolution and a proletarian revolution in all countries though we have suggested one

---

57. See Gouldner, op.cit., Theses Eleven and Fourteen, pp. 57-75 and pp. 83-85.

reading of Marx which could deny the need for the former, at least, in some parts of the world. This essentially was the starting point of the studies of Moore and Konrad and Szelenyi. Outside the Marxist framework we have considered a number of different characterisations of the revolutions which have led to modernity. Varients of Burnham's managerial revolution may be found in the work of Galbraith and Gouldner. Even further from Marx one might follow Sorokin in noting that the term modernisation is culture-specific and 'ideational' modernisation might be a very different thing from 'sensate' modernisation. According to that view, the major revolutions in history have been the shift from one type of culture to another. Now as we face the 'age of Aquarius' we are confronted with the advent of a new 'ideational' revolution.

Perhaps most controversy arises when one considers the necessity for revolution in the sense of the overthrow of regimes by collective violence. If one takes Marx's 'premise of history' that humans are basically productive and co-operative beings and if, like Bakunin or Fanon, one believes in the psychological function of violence to liberate the repressed or alienated person, then clearly the answer is affirmative. If, moreover, one believes in the intransigent nature of ruling classes doomed to destruction, then one would arrive at the same answer; though Marx himself did envisage the possibility of a proletarian revolution in Britain, Holland and America proceeding non-violently. Perhaps one would agree with Wertheim that the violent overthrow of regimes is not absolutely necessary to every modernisation process but is so likely as to make the question rather ridiculous. Or perhaps, like Moore, one is content to note that there has been no major society in east nor west which has not undergone a violent revolution in the course of its modernisation and in each case the violent overthrow of the ancien regime involved less human suffering that the regime it replaced. Whether Moore or opponents such as Brinton or Sorokin are correct on this issue is not just an empirical question; at root must be a theory of exactly what constitutes human suffering.

Most people in most ages who are not caught up in the turmoil of violent revolution act as though they were at the end of history. Stability is usually taken to be the norm despite the voluminous evidence produced by Sorokin and any appeal to sound historical common sense. The principle of induction may be flawed philosophically but without it social science would not be possible. We believe that one can predict the occurrence of violent revolutions in the industrialised world with some degree of confidence. But who can be sure where they will start? Will they originate with Marcuse's 'marginal people' or will they eventuate from the 'fatal flaw' in Gouldner's new class? And will they all lead to proletarian revolution? As Marx saw them the contradictions of the capitalist system could lead to communism or the mutual destruction of the contending classes. In the context of the present arms race, the latter scenario looks quite likely. Yet does the future depend upon that ultimate instrument of diffusion - the multiple warhead missile - or will that be merely one of Johnson's 'accelerators' which will activate prior cleavages in what may be left of society.

2.

MODERNISATION AND REVOLUTION IN THE THIRD WORLD

The preceding chapter discussed several conceptions of modernisation in relation to three types of revolution - cultural, political economic and narrowly political. The aim was to examine how industrialised countries got to be the way they are and the role of revolution in that process. This chapter will extend the argument to a discussion of the academic treatment of revolution in the contemporary third world.

What then is the third world and how does it relate to the other two? Twenty years ago it could plausibly be argued that the first world consisted of the industrialised capitalist countries, the second world was the 'socialist camp' and the third world was the remainder. Since then the socialist camp has split. China, asserting its hostility to the Soviet Union, has redefined the world in terms of power, with both the United States and the Soviet Union in the first world, other industrialised capitalist and self-proclaimed socialist states in the second and China plus the rest in the third. It might also be argued, with the decline in American power in the 1970s and the replacement of the dollar as the paramount medium of international exchange, that the capitalist world is also fragmenting. It seems odd, moreover, to place Bangladesh (a very poor country) in the same category as Taiwan (a country with remarkable indicators of economic growth) or China (a huge country containing one quarter of the world's population) in the same category as Singapore (a city state). The term third world covers a vast range of economic profiles, rates of economic growth and military power. Would it not be more sensible to talk about rich and poor, strong and weak, capitalist and socialist countries? If we were to do that, however, we might finish up with as many categories as there are states. In our view it makes a lot of sense to bracket together and assign a name to countries with widespread poverty, low bargaining power in the international market, high vulnerability to global economic fluctuations, minimal social services and the like. We do this, however, in the full knowledge that the boundaries are fuzzy and that there are countries that do not fit easily into our categorisation. We excuse our imprecision on the grounds that the alternative - an examination in terms of different scales of achievement - might hide the international and domestic cleavages which are among the primary causes of revolution.

Nevertheless, since so many accounts of development are cast in terms of such scales (e.g. per capita gross national product, the development of 'modern' institutions, the growth of 'modern' types of behaviour), we must start our discussion with such accounts. These, in fact, constituted the orthodoxy of development thinkers during the 1950s and 1960s. They tended to see change as the result of diffusion of 'modern' ideas and institutions from the first world and revolution (in all three senses outlined in the previous chapter) in terms of problems of personal or institutional adjustment to what had been diffused. Evolution was the ideal to be pursued by all development planners. We will then go on to discuss an alternative view - that of dependency - which became fashionable in the late 1960s and early 1970s. This saw the influence of the first world on the third not as beneficial but as very harmful and provided a mirror image of the first view. Here revolution was cast in terms of withdrawal from the global system. Finally we shall examine attempts to move beyond the above two views, looking at recent accounts of the problems of modernisation in parts of the third world and consider the implications for revolution.

The Diffusionist Orthodoxy : Diffusion and Modernity

Though multilinear approaches to development were never totally eclipsed in the 'long boom' of the 1950s and 1960s, it is fair to say that the orthodoxy of development thinkers was both technologically determinist and ethnocentric. The technological determinist orientation found its clearest expression in W.W. Rostow's classic The Stages of Economic Growth[58] which saw third world countries as participating in a kind of air-race in which they moved to a take-off position, after which self-sustained growth became possible. Such a view suggested that investment by first world countries in the third world helped provide the conditions for 'take-off', and that revolution directed against foreign domination was economically irrational. This work, subtitled A Non-Communist Manifesto was immensely influential amongst those who considered that revolution in the third world was the work of malevolent communists. Such communists, it was believed, exported revolution to the underdeveloped countries and seduced local people with Lenin's view that it was only by sending capital to the third world that developed capitalist countries maintained their high standard of living. Both the air race model and the idea that revolution is exported seem dubious. Countries do not just take off after the appropriate infusion of technology and then remain flying. Some take off and then crash (e.g. Poland). Others never reach the end of the runway and are denied entry into a crowded sky, whilst a few provide models of growth for economists committed to 'the magic of the market' (e.g. Taiwan and South Korea). Doubtless revolutions in some third world countries (in the narrowly political sense) were provoked by foreign intervention (e.g. the three countries of Indo China) but the receptiveness of those countries to revolutionary ideas depended to a large extent on the domestic situation and the prospect of a revolution in the wider political economy sense. In any case, it is extremely difficult to argue that foreign influence was at all significant amongst the revolutionaries who overthrew the Shah of Iran.

The above picture is one of diffusion. Technology is diffused from the west to facilitate the conditions for take off. But diffusion of technology from the west is accompanied by the spread of 'modern' western cultural values which might be resisted in third world countries. It is possible, therefore, that revolutions in the political sense of the word might actually be the product, not of external subversion, but of that very resistence. Attempts to explain such a phenomenon often draw upon the structural-functionalist framework of analysis discussed in the previous chapter in connection with the work of Chalmers Johnson. The structural-functionalist framework, it will be remembered, started from the assumption that human beings rationally pursue their common human needs within structures dictated by the environment. Those social structures develop to perform a number of functions necessary to reproduce the social system. They do this by fostering 'orientations to action' on the part of

---

58.   Rostow, W.W., The Stages of Economic Growth: A Non-Communist Manifesto, Cambridge University Press, 1962.

individuals. When the environment changes due to the diffusion of goods, values etc. from more advanced societies, the necessary social functions may only be fulfilled by the attainment of a new equilibrium between social institutions and orientations to action. A revolution, therefore, will occur when the gradual attainment of the new equilibrium is frustrated. The previous chapter has already explained some of the problems attending this view. First the argument is circular. Secondly, since functions have meaning only in terms of stability, revolutions can only be seen as aberrant cases of mal-adaptation to the inexorable dictates of diffused modernisation; or to put it another way revolutions in the narrowly political sense of the word are merely the consequences of badly-managed cultural evolution.

According to the above view, cultural evolution is defined ethnocentrically. Thus Pye, talking about the pace and scope of social change in South East Asia, argued that it was dependent upon the extent to which colonial rulers established

1.   rationalised administrative practices.
2.   fixed and standardised taxation in place of tribute in kind, corvee labour etc.
3.   secular and codified legal systems.
4.   liberal economic policies.
5.   a westernised education system.[59]

The 'new images of authority' which derived from the above were clearly of western origin as indeed was the very conception of rationality itself. What was usually meant by 'rational' in such discussions was the choice of means appropriate to ends which were self evident. It seemed obvious that promotion of persons on the basis of technical achievement was better than on the basis of family relationships[60]. What was ignored was the fact that economic development was often better served by ties of kinship or quasi-kinship. This had surely been the case among Jewish, Lebanese or Overseas Chinese communities. Indeed, part of Japan's economic 'miracle' was achieved within networks of quasi-kinship. What was ignored in the whole debate was a very different kind of rationality oriented towards values which might derive from an ideal society or perhaps from the stock of cultural symbols rooted in particular local traditions. It was by no means self-evident, therefore, that religious ties between local elites and the masses would disappear as industrialisation proceeded. They might actually be reinforced as people became oriented towards different aspects of traditional cultural symbols. This is what happened in the Protestant Reformation in the west (God, the author of a rational and well ordered universe, was transformed into God the unknowable who might only be approached by faith). Why shouldn't the same kind of process occur in countries like Iran? It is quite ethnocentric to argue that the recent religious revivals are simply throwbacks to a tradition which ought to have

---

59.   Pye, Lucian, 'The Politics of Southeast Asia', in Almond, G.A. and Coleman, J.S. (eds.), The Politics of the Developing Areas, Princeton University Press, 1960, p. 84.

60.   ibid., pp. 82-152.

been discarded. As Wertheim points out, religion is not always the opium of the people. It may be a powerful stimulant.

Failure to predict the recent Islamic revolutions, it seems, stems from a fundamental flaw in the diffusionists' approach. They all acknowledge that change and adaptation proceeds unevenly. But the problem is not just one of a lack of fit between social structure and 'orientations to action'. Fundamental dislocation may occur within both social structure and 'orientations to action'. Thus, as Lucien Pye noted, one of the consequences of westernisation was the drive for administrative centralisation. The growth of cities in many third world countries was not the result of industrialisation, as in the west, but of a change in administrative activities. The growth of urbanisation at a rate much faster than industrialisation was to generate social tensions which frustrated another goal of westernisation - the efficient deployment of resources to achieve a rise across the board in the standard of living. The adoption of one form of structural change from the west, therefore, militated against another; and it was not much use castigating third world leaders for being 'unsystematic'. Should one be surprised, therefore, at the recent urban revolution in Iran, which combines a rational rejection of the source of frustration with what westerners claim to be an irrational affirmation of Islamic fundamentalism? Surely only an armchair academic could complain that Islamic revolutionaries should be more discriminating in what was being rejected.

The fact that different aspects of the western notion of modernisation may come into contradiction with each other makes it extremely difficult for the diffusionist to evaluate the degree of modernisation achieved. A country might rank quite high on one western scale of modernisation (e.g. 'economic development') and quite low on another ('political development'). Such a country, we might suggest, is South Korea. Within each scale of development, moreover, there are insuperable contradictions. Is an oil rich state with amongst the highest per capita GNPs in the world but with minimal social services developed economically? And when it comes to political development, the problems seem even greater. Some two decades ago Gabriel Almond, a pioneer in that field, attempted to develop a list of functional categories within which to chart the progression of a polity from tradition to modernity. These included political socialisation (making people aware of politics), interest articulation (the ability to voice particular interests), interest aggregation (the formation of parties, pressure groups etc.) and political communication. It should be possible, he believed, to chalk up progress in each of these 'input' functions and then look at the 'output' functions of rule making (legislative), rule application (executive) and rule adjudication (judicial). A developed polity would be one which displayed a high degree of structural differentiation within a bureaucracy which processed the input functions and serviced the output functions.[61] Almond's pioneering work spawned many books which used these functional categories. But the problem remained! If one accepts the ethnocentric view how does one explain how a low score on one functional category might be combined with a high score

---

61. Almond, G.A., 'Introduction: A Functional Approach to Comparative Politics', in Almond, G.A. and Coleman, J.S. (eds.), op.cit., pp. 3-64.

on another, especially when both scores might be generated by the same process? The Indian revolution, for example, (if, as Wertheim claims, that is what it was), produced a polity which performed quite well in terms of input functions but displayed a completely contradictory performance in terms of output. It now possesses a rather inept legislature which periodically passes acts that it does not expect to see enforced, a well differentiated bureaucracy, and an executive which from time to time overwhelms both legislature and judiciary and usually gets away with it.

Cultural Diffusion and Revolution

Nowadays little is said about the functional categories pioneered by Almond. What is left of the structural-functionalist paradigm is the argument concerning adaptation to what is diffused from the west, though now much greater sophistication may be found in explicit discussions of revolution. Take for example the work of Samuel Huntington who argues that revolution as a form of collective violence is one product of the diffusion of modern ideas into a situation where the regime is incapable of developing institutions adequate to contain the strain.[62] Where institutionalisation does occur and collective violence is avoided we have 'development'; but where modernisation fails to be complemented by institutionalisation, we have 'political decay'. For Huntington:

> The political essence of revolution is the rapid expansion of political consciousness and the rapid mobilization of new groups into politics at a speed which makes it impossible for existing political institutions to assimilate them.[63]

Thus, revolution as a form of collective violence is not a product of 'traditional' society, nor of 'modern' industrialised society, but of societies in the early stages of modernisation. Such a view, it is said, contradicts the picture painted by Marx.[64] Modern revolutions in the 'east', moreover, take a form very different from those which occurred in the west during its early modernisation. In the 'east', new groups mobilise outside the old order and then move in to overthrow it; whereas in the west the old institutions had to disintegrate before new groups mobilised and entered politics.

Whatever the level of sophistication reached, it seems impossible to escape from the tautologies which the last chapter noted in the discussion of Johnson. Huntington's tautology is quite apparent; revolution and

---

62. Huntington, S., Political Order in Changing Societies, Yale University Press, New Haven, 1968. Also see Huntington, S., 'Political Development and Political Decay, World Politics, Vol. 17, No. 3, 1965.

63. Huntington, Political Order..., p. 266.

64. Tucker, R., The Marxian Revolutionary Idea, Norton, New York, 1969 pp. 136-7.

modernisation are defined in terms of each other.[65] Thus, all Huntington is saying is that revolutions occur except when existing institutions prevent them. The very word 'institutionalisation' is defined in terms of the absence of revolution. Secondly we are never quite sure which elements of modernisation are decisive in causing instability. Could it be rapid urbanisation which we advanced earlier as a factor in the Iranian revolution? Huntington, it appears, does not seem to think so since the lumpenproletariat which lives on the fringes of modernising cities is hardly ever a force for radical change.[66] Could it be disorientation caused by unfamiliarity with industrial routine? Surely that also cannot be the case; at most such a condition causes machine breaking and other Luddite activities which hardly ever constitute a challenge to the political regime. Could it be the poor working conditions which normally pertain in the early stages of industrialisation? Again, such an explanation is unlikely since major upheavals usually occur after the promulgation of some factory legislation. We are left, therefore, with no explanation as to why political mobilisation becomes effective other than the point, made long ago by Marx, that modern industry collects people together in numbers larger than ever before.

As for the claim that Marx has been refuted by the observation that revolutions occur in the early stages of modernisation, enough was said in the previous chapter to demonstrate that Marx was talking about proletarian revolution in the political-economy sense. Under most circumstances, Marx gave reasons as to why this would be violent, but did allow for the possibility of non-violent revolution in Britain, Holland and America. Such could be achieved because of the cultural traditions of those countries and the weakness of the military-bureaucratic apparatus within them.[67] In any case, no revolution in the contemporary third world might be described as proletarian in the sense in which Marx understood the term. Neither was the Russian revolution of 1917 nor the Chinese revolution, which culminated in 1949, proletarian. As Lenin saw it, socialism or even state control over a capitalist economy was something to be established in the future[68] and the Chinese revolution was predicated on the leadership of a 'four class bloc' (workers, peasants, national bourgeoisie

---

65.   A useful discussion of Huntington's tautological approach and his use of evidence is Tilly, C., 'Does Modernization Breed Revolution', Comparative Politics, Vol. V, No. 3, April 1973, pp. 359-92.

66.   Huntington, op.cit., p. 278.

67.   Marx. K., (1872) in H. Gerth (ed.), The First International: Minutes of the Hague Congress of 1972 with Related Documents, University of Wisconsin Press, Madison, 1958, p. 236.

68.   Lenin, V., '"Left Wing" Childishness and the Petty Bourgeois Mentality', May 1918, in Lenin, V., Selected Works, 3 Vol. edn., Progress Publishers, Moscow, 1976, Vol. II, pp. 631-7.

and petty bourgeosie).[69] Huntington's mistake is to conflate Marx's broader (political economy) conception of revolution with the narrow political definition in terms of the overthrow of a regime by collective violence. Secondly he ignores Marx's argument that the tradition of particular countries will affect the possibility of violence. Finally, Huntington's conclusion about the 'eastern' and 'western' types of revolution is highly questionable. The 1911 revolution in China, for example, conforms more to the western pattern whereas that which culminated in 1949 is a clear case of the eastern type. Using Huntington's formula one could also conclude that the American revolution after 1776 was of the eastern type. A Marxist might, of course, disqualify the Chinese revolution of 1911 and the American revolution of 1776 on the ground that in neither did the mode of production change. Huntington, however, is not a Marxist, and since he defines revolution in the narrow (collective violence) and cultural senses of the word, he is obliged to take such revolutions seriously.

Cultural Diffusion and Social Psychology

What is missing from Huntington's analysis is an adequate theory linking the political, the economic and the psychological. Huntington attempts to establish a linkage by starting from the political dimension. W.W. Rostow, on the other hand, starts from the economic dimension. In the first case the result is tautological thinking, and in the second a rather crude economic determinism. A third, and at first sight more attractive, approach is to start from considerations of social psychology.

The late development of social psychological approaches to revolution often blinds us to the fact that attempts have been made in this direction since the time of Aristotle.[70] In modern times, long before people began to think in terms of the third world, Alexis de Tocqueville offered us an interesting psychological dimension in his analysis of the great French Revolution.[71] As he saw it, revolution in the political economy sense was well under way before the events of 1789-95. Under the royal absolutism of the Bourbon regime there had already taken place a massive transfer of economic and political power to the bourgeoisie. What remained was aristocratic privilege without much power. The general rise in affluence in the eighteenth century consequent upon the transfer of power to the bourgeoisie, moreover, produced a rising horizon of expectations which allowed those who already had considerable power to see that they could easily destroy aristocratic privilege. To this Tocqueville added the general psychological postulate that greater resentment is felt by those who have some power and little privilege than by those who have no power and no privilege.

---

69. Mao Zedong, 'On New Democracy', January 1940, Selected Works, Foreign Languages Press, Beijing, 1965, Vol. II, pp. 339-84.

70. Aristotle, The Politics (ed. E. Barker) Oxford University Press, 1948, Book V.

71. De Tocqueville, A., The Ancien Regime and the French Revolution (1856), Collins/Fontana, 1966.

The psychological consequences of a lack of fit between power and privilege, we would suggest, are quite apparent in third world countries in the early stages of westernisation. In Latin America, the phenomenon of 'the middle class military coup' occurs when a powerful westernised section of an army comes to resent the government of traditional caudillos (military leaders) based on the privileges of land ownership. Such also has been the pattern of the Egyptian and other Middle Eastern revolutions. The need, however, is to specify the link between social position and psychological orientation.

In recent years attempts to achieve this have taken the form of a number of theses about 'relative deprivation'. The earliest of these were not set within a specifically third world context and were outside the context of theories of diffusion. They were, however, meant to be valid for all societies and have increasingly been incorporated into the general literature on development. Such an early attempt was that of James Davies the originator of the 'J curve' thesis.[72] This holds that a growing awareness of the benefits of economic growth produces a 'rising horizon of expectations'. This horizon of expectations continues to rise even when an economic slump occurs. The result is a gap between expectations and achievement which causes resentment. When that resentment is directed at a regime, revolution is likely.

Though one may argue that the French and Russian revolutions might be seen in terms of frustrated expectations, one cannot fail to observe that the 'J curve' phenomenon was evident in most countries in the world during the great depression of the 1930s: yet few revolutions in fact occurred. Davies' attempt to explain this situation casts doubt on his whole approach. A revolution did not occur during the 1930s in the United States, he tells us, because of 'the vigor with which the national government attacked the depression in 1933'.[73] Does that mean that a revolutionary response to the 'J curve' occurs only when governments are too weak to take any remedial action and are held responsible by people for their economic plight? If such is the case, the 'J curve' thesis is no more than one factor amongst many which might explain why people and groups become disaffected with governments. There is also a problem of evidence. Many cases might be cited of societies in the 1930s which avoided revolutions even though significant portions of the population blamed their weak governments for failure to respond to the depression. A similar position, we would contend, pertains today in both the advanced industrial and the third worlds. In the latter, the overwhelming majority of countries are currently in a 'J curve' situation; yet world revolution seems remote.

Perhaps one of the most telling arguments against Davies' formulation of the 'J curve' thesis, when applied to the third world, is provided by Wertheim. He argues that in the third world the horizon of expectations tends to be class-specific. Though the horizon of expectations of bourgeois groups might rise with the beginnings of economic growth, peasant expectations can remain static or decline. In any case, the question of

72.   Davies, J. 'Towards a Theory of Revolution', American Sociological Review, Vol. XXVII, No. 1, 1962, pp. 5-19.

73.   ibid., p. 17.

expectations is much more complex than the 'J curve' thesis allows. In Java, for example, the depression of the 1930s caused a decline in the expectations of the Indonesian bourgeoisie, which was only reversed when the Japanese occupying power replaced Dutch officials by Indonesians, to whom it offered a kind of independence. It was the return of the Dutch which brought about the decline in achievement and the 'J curve' phenomenon. Meanwhile the expectations of peasants, declining during the depression, continued to decline throughout the whole period of Japanese occupation.[74] Wertheim's point is well made: no theory which attempts to reconcile expectations with achievement is much use unless one takes into account class division. In other words one has to link social psychological explanations with arguments about social structure.

We can think of no single study where that link between a sociological and a social psychological approach has been adequately forged. In fact the tendency has been for the two approaches to diverge; though, to be sure, both have become much more sophisticated since Davies' first article and the work of Chalmers Johnson. In the field of social psychology the Feierabends and Nesvold have created a number of interesting variations of the 'J curve' thesis,[75] Ted Gurr has enumerated a typology of relative deprivation which specifies two basic categories of relative deprivation additional to Davies' initial model.[76] The first of these describes the potential for collective violence stemming from the gap between a rising horizon of expectations and a capability (that which can be achieved) which remains static (aspirational deprivation). Such a situation is extremely common in newly independent countries which expect far too much from the independent regime. The second form of deprivation (decremental) arises when people become increasingly unable to satisfy stable expectations. This, for Sorokin, was the general cause of all revolutions.[77] In the third world, it is felt typically by a 'traditional' elite displaced by a colonial authority. An additional pattern, suggested by Hagopian, occurs when rising expectations outstrip rising capabilities (accelerated deprivation). Such a situation may have held at the time of the Meiji restoration (in 1869), which Moore considered to be a revolution. Indeed anyone with imagination may create further models specifying the relationship between expectations and capabilities. Suppose, for example, that declining capabilities outstrip declining expectations. Could this have been the motivation of the pro-Vietnamese groups in Pol Pot's Kampuchea? To all this one might add the methodology pioneered by the Feierabends which poses

----

74.   Wertheim, op.cit., pp. 191-7. When referring to the bourgeoisie, Wertheim speaks of a 'reversed J curve'.

75.   I. Feierabend, R. Feierabend and B. Nesvold, 'Social Change and Political Violence: Cross-National Patterns' in Graham, H. and Gurr, T. (eds.), The History of Violence in America: Historical and Comparative Perspectives, Praeger, New York, 1969, pp. 637-44.

76.   Gurr, T., Why Men Rebel, Princeton University Press, 1970, pp.46-56. Gurr refers to Davies' pattern as 'progressive deprivation'.

77.   Sorokin, P., The Sociology of Revolution, op.cit., 1967, pp. 367-9.

hypotheses about the rate at which the relative deprivation gap appears and the degree of fluctuations of both capabilities and expectations.[78] But however complicated the picture becomes, the methodological problems of forging an adequate link between the sociological and the social psychological approach are immense.

First, how is it possible for the social psychologist to explain the conditions under which the potential for collective violence becomes translated into revolution rather than anything else? Second, it seems useless to talk about relative deprivation unless one specifies just what one means by capabilities and expectations. Various schemes have been put forward. The crudest simply measures actual income, makes guesses about potential income and asks a sample about expected income. At a more sophisticated level, variations of Abraham Maslow's hierarchy of needs are employed. Maslow listed five categories of universal needs with the following priority, (1) physiological needs, (2) safety needs, (3) affection needs, (4) esteem needs and (5) self actualisation or self development needs.[79] Each of these need areas become activated only when the prior needs are met; but once a higher need becomes activated it is not necessarily extinguished when the individual suffers deprivation of a prior need. It is according to Maslow's scheme that Davies argues that the satisfaction of physical needs may lead to a feeling of deprivation with regard to other needs and so on.[80] A revolution, therefore, may depend upon frustration at any of the above levels. Such a theory sounds quite plausible until one considers how one could ascertain at the social level when needs 3, 4 or 5 are contributing to violence. Alexis de Tocqueville tied together the lack of bourgeois esteem and the French revolution, and Frantz Fanon saw violence as a precursor of self-development. But how one could establish the association empirically remains an open question. The situation is even further complicated when one considers what causes expectations to rise. Perhaps a fruitful line of enquiry is to examine the various expectations of modernising groups (bureaucrats, merchants) who are apparently in a position to appropriate the wealth or power of traditional elites or classes. But if that is our scenario, we have no need for social psychology. A simple explanation of group conflict based on rational calculation would provide an adequate account.

In our view, Wertheim's own attempt to reconcile politics, economics and psychology in an explanation of revolution in terms of collective violence appears quite fruitful. As he sees them, the regimes created by departing colonial powers are usually based on time-honoured patron-client relations. The basic ideology of such regimes is a form of 'populism' (a petty-bourgeois cum peasant ideology which posits the existence of an

78.   Feierabend, Feierabend and Nesvold, loc.cit., pp. 632-87.

79.   Maslow, A., Motivation and Personality, 2nd ed., Harper and Row, New York, 1954. pp. 35-47.
       To the five needs listed Maslow then added 'the desire to know and understand' and 'aesthetic needs', see ibid., pp. 48-58.

80.   Davies, J., 'The J-curve of Rising and Declining Satisfaction as a cause of some great Revolutions and a contained Rebellion', in Graham and Gurr (eds.), op.cit., pp. 690-730.

undifferentiated 'people', led usually by a charismatic leader). Such was the case in Indonesia and most countries on the African continent. These regimes have a low potential for violent revolution, and the patron-client relations are a powerful conservative force. To accommodate many different groups, however, some of which are Marxist (though similarly based on patron-client relations), the modernising regimes adopt a 'left' posture, which makes them vulnerable to the retaliation of vested interests and the American practitioners of counter-revolution (defined in terms of his emancipation principle). Though revolution can never be exported, counter-revolution may be, and the Americans are past masters of the art. The result is usually the establishment of military dictatorships which destroy patron-client relations by force. That, Wertheim believes, is what happened in the Indonesian counter-revolution of 1965. The masses, destabilised by such a situation, easily turn to guerila groups which provide a new sense of solidarity and offer the only way of furthering emancipation.[81]

Though we are somewhat sceptical about the recent contributions of social psychology towards an understanding of revolutions in the third world, we cannot deny that the arguments of social psychologists were taken very seriously by those who wished to prevent violent revolutions. Social psychology was, after all, a major element in Project Camelot - the abortive attempt by the United States government to analyse the cause of violent revolution in the 1960s.[82] Such projects are no longer fashionable nor considered cost-effective. In the meantime, regimes attempt to prevent violent revolution in third world countries by using policies which Wertheim considers of little use. In his view, economic and welfare measures rarely go far enough: psychological distractions can last only for a short time; and repression by brute force can easily become a revolutionary accelerator[83].

The Dependency Paradigm: A Challenge to the Diffusionists?

The diffusionist paradigm regarded revolution as the result of maladaptation to a Western conception of the march of progress. Such maladaptation might be seen as stemming from uneven development (e.g. urbanisation without economic growth, the formation of political parties without institutions to contain them etc.) or from different kinds of 'relative deprivation'. The need to include the political, the economic and the psychological in an explanation of revolution is now widely accepted, though we have argued that the prospect for synthesis offered by the discipline of social psychology is far from satisfactory. But what other disciplinary perspective might help us towards a synthesis? As we have seen, the contribution of political science towards an understanding of 'political development' is now regarded as outdated. Rostow's 'air race' is

81.   Wertheim, op.cit., pp. 236-64.

82.   See Horowitz, I.L., (ed.), The Rise and Fall of Project Camelot, The MIT Press, Massachusetts, Revised edition, 1974.

83.   Wertheim, op.cit., pp. 265-95.

highly questionable and structural functionalist sociology has dissolved in a morass of tautologies.

By the mid-1960s, a new perspective appeared within the discipline of political economy. At that time the recognition that many third world countries might not be in a position to 'catch-up' with the advanced industrial nations, led to a rejection by many of the diffusionist paradigm. There began to develop what were known as 'dependency' theories which held that there was a necessary relationship between development and underdevelopment. A pioneer in this work was the economist Andre Gunder Frank[84] who argued, from a study of Latin America, that part of the economic surplus of countries occupying the 'periphery' of the international capitalist system was extracted by countries at the 'core'. Those 'peripheral' countries, dependent upon the metropolitan capitalist countries, were to be seen as 'passive victims'. Their history was not in the least autonomous. It was determined by their position in a single world capitalist economy. This dependency, however, was not considered to be a one-sided relationship. The metropolitan capitalist countries had needed peripheral countries to assist in the task of capital accumulation in the past and continued to need them to overcome economic stagnation. The same historical process which had generated development at the core had also generated underdevelopment in the periphery. This process continued into the monopoly stage of capitalism with the third world providing investment outlets for the expanded surplus expropriated by the metropoles.

The picture painted was of an all-pervading capitalist system of control ranging down from the metropoles through the capital cities of satellite nations to regional and local centres, then through the large landowners and merchants to the small peasants, tenants and landless labourers.[85] The extraction of the surplus proceeded in the opposite direction with each level appropriating a portion of the surplus. Such a picture seemed attractive to revolutionaries in the 1960s in that a revolutionary dislocation at any point in the system could be seen as contributing to a global revolution in the political economy sense. It helped to explain why the United States was prepared to spend countless times more money on suppressing the Vietnamese revolution than it could ever recover from that area; what was at stake was the entire system of capitalist control. Yet at the same time, in the absence of 'many Vietnams'

---

84. Frank has been described as a Chicago-trained economist who experienced 'a road to Damascus' conversion on first visiting Latin America. See Foster-Carter, A., 'Neo-Marxist Approaches to Development and Under-development', in Journal of Contemporary Asia, Vol. 3, No. 1, 1973, pp. 7-33.

85. The most celebrated, reproduced (and criticised) essay in which Frank sets out his position is 'The Development of Underdevelopment'. It appears as the opening essay in Frank, A.G., Latin America: Under-Development or Revolution, Monthly Review Press, New York, 1969, pp. 3-17. Other Frank contributions during the 1960s included 'On the Mechanisms of Imperialism: The Case of Brazil', Monthly Review, Vol. 16, No. 5, 1964. 'Services Rendered', Monthly Review, Vol. 17, No. 2, 1965, Capitalism and Underdevelopment, Monthly Review Press, New York, 1969.

(a constant theme of Che Guevara) the theory pointed to the futility of a revolution aimed at nationalising foreign assets in an economy skewed to the export of one or two crops or mineral resources. Whatever regime might take power would find its economic activities constrained by the international system. Frank's diagnosis, therefore, seemed to suggest that nothing short of instant world revolution would achieve very much. In the 1970s, when that eventuality seemed very remote, Frank's paradigm became accepted by very respectable elites in third world countries as a rationale for their inability to achieve the economic growth they had promised on taking power.

While we would not want to deny the distorting and blocking effects of foreign penetration in the third world, we are not convinced that Frank's arguments about capital flow are useful. Even if it can be demonstrated that there is, in fact, a net outflow of capital from the third to the first worlds, it is probably much too small to have any significant effect on the prospects for development. What is important, from an economic point of view, is not so much the international flow of profits but the productivity of capital which remains in third world countries.

A second major criticism of Frank's original thesis is that arguments about the international division of labour tended to crowd out considerations of the class structure of individual third world countries. Responding to such criticism, Frank was later to attempt an integration of class analysis with his thesis about the international division of labour. An analysis of the class structure of Latin American countries, he concluded, pointed to the fact that objective conditions did not exist for any nationalist or autonomous solution to the problems of development. All over the continent one saw the growth of what he called a lumpenbourgeoisie - a class formed in response to the needs of foreign industry and commerce which was interested in keeping the people in a state of wretched backwardness. Instead of all-round development one had lumpendevelopment which reproduced the conditions whereby that class remained dominant.[86]

In a situation characterised as lumpendevelopment revolutions would only occur when the hold of the metropolitan capitalist powers was weakened. Such had been the pattern in past revolutions in Latin America. The revolutions which had brought many of the various states into existence at the beginning of the nineteenth century had become possible when the power of Spain collapsed before Napoleon's armies. At that time landed interests utilised the ideology of liberalism to wrest power from colonial authorities. In the twentieth century, the great depression of the 1930s and the war in Europe provided opportunities for revolutions led by indigenous bourgeois elements. Here Frank was talking about revolutions in the political economy sense of the word. They were clearly different from the incessant coups d'etat which had dogged most of recent Latin American history. Such political-economic revolutions did not necessitate the violent overthrow of regimes as is exemplified in the most famous Mexican revolution led by Cardenas. In fact, the manifestation of widespread violence quite often resulted not from revolutionary insurrections but from interests allied with foreign powers fomenting

---

86.   See Frank, A.G., Lumpenbourgeoisie, Lumpendevelopment, Monthly Review Press, New York, 1972.

counter-revolution. Such has been a repeated occurrence in Argentina where, paradoxically, the one regime, which did offer prospects of an autonomous revolution in the political economy sense, came to power expressing sympathy for European fascism.

The above arguments about Latin America, it would seem, have relevance for recent revolutions in other parts of the world. Few would deny that the decline of European power in Asia during the Second World War fostered the development of revolutionary forces in many countries, though in Africa south of the Sahara the situation was very different - due perhaps to the lack of development at that time of a bourgeoisie committed to autonomy. In the 1950s and 1960s, however, the assertion of American power made such 'national capitalist' revolutions highly unlikely. In Latin America there was only Velasco's Peruvian revolution (1968) which was unable to carry through the seizure of power into a revolution in the political economy sense. In Asia, U Ne Win's Burmese revolution seemed only to condemn that country to perpetual stagnation. For Frank and many dependency theorists like him, autonomous capitalist development through revolution seems no longer on the agenda.

The work of Frank pointed to the need for development thinkers to look at the world as a whole and, amongst the dependency theorists, the most outstanding achievement in this regard was the work of Immanuel Wallerstein.[87] Wallerstein began by asking why the European core was able to develop before the rest of the world. The conventional diffusionist view held that the commercialisation of agriculture in Britain, which drove peasants off the land, provided both capital for industrial investment and a proletariat to work in industrial enterprises. The growth generated by this development then served as a model for the rest of the world. Wallerstein accepted the first part of this view but severely modified the second. As he saw it the commercialisation of agriculture in the seventeenth century coincided with a period where the 'second serfdom' east of the Elbe had tied peasants to the land. Soon the west was in a position to sell industrial goods at relatively high prices to the east in return for lower priced grain. Thus, the 'core' capitalist countries profited at the expense of Russia and Eastern Europe which at that time constituted the periphery. The same process has continued to this day with the periphery getting bigger and bigger. Such development has resulted in a complicated global division of labour in which a new category - the 'semi-periphery' - has appeared. Each of these three zones performs different economic roles in maintaining the global capitalist system. Each zone is characterised by a different mode of labour control, a different pattern of profit generation and a different class structure. With the growth of this division of labour, there has developed a system of state power in which core states appear very strong due to the need by capitalists for 'extra-economic assistance' to secure favourable terms of trade. At the periphery, on the other hand, the strength of states ranges from negligibility (in the colonial situation) to a very low level (under conditions of neo-colonialism). Such a global division of labour and geographical division of power, which has developed over four centuries, is extremely stable and

---

87. Wallerstein, Immanuel, The Modern World-System: Capitalist Agriculture and the Origins of the European World - Economy in the Sixteenth Century, Academic Press, New York and London, 1974.

might be expected to remain stable so long as the market is able to expand into areas in which pre-capitalist forms of economy exist.

After the discussion in the preceding chapter it will be quite apparent that the above is based on a very selective reading of history. Wallerstein argued that successful market relations at the 'core' led to the development of strong states to protect and further develop market relations. In the periphery, however, the failure successfully to develop market relations precluded the development of strong states. Such an argument ignores the pre-existing state structures in the periphery. Konrad and Szelenyi, it will be remembered, based their whole argument on the fact that it required a very strong state (in what Wallerstein calls the periphery) to bring about the 'second serfdom' in the first place. With such evidence, how is it possible to argue that the unequal strength of state structures is necessary to sustain the global division of labour? In Konrad and Szelenyi's analysis the strength of the eastern states was a decisive force in bringing about an alternative path to modernisation. With Wallerstein we are back to the same ethnocentric and unilinear view as that offerred by the diffusionists. In Wallerstein's thesis revolutions in the narrow political sense are merely the consequence of the mal-adaptation of peripheral societies to the demands of the metropoles. Though Wallerstein's picture does allow for a more sophisticated analysis of class formations, classes are reduced merely to categories in a world market system. There is an absence of pressure or action from below. All change has ultimately to flow from the preferences of the dominant classes in 'core' capitalist nations.

Is not this the mirror image of the diffusionist paradigm? [88] All that has changed is the observer's moral evaluation of the consequences of a top-down view of progress. The trickle-down benefits are now reinterpreted as patterns of exploitation. The plusses of the diffusionist view have simply become the minuses of the dependency view. And what of revolution in the political economy sense? Can one conceive of a set of occurrences which will bring the system to an end? Could it be that the same structure of world power, established in the sixteenth century, will be maintained so long as the market can expand? And when the market covers the whole globe and there are no more traditional producers to fleece, will the system collapse and usher in a revolutionary age?

A Return to Internal Dynamics: Revolution as 'Violence' that is to be Avoided.

By the late 1970s, the attention of many students of the world economy had switched to the problem of resources. Some people argued that for the whole world to enjoy the contemporary standard of living of

---

88.   Here we are in agreement with Theda Skocpol. Her argument
       is that any attempt to create a new paradigm, through discreet,
       polemic opposition to an old one, is 'plagued' by the 'the mirror
       image trap', i.e. 'innovators uncritically carry over outmoded
       theoretical categories...and if they define new ones (they do so)
       mainly by searching for the seemingly direct opposite of the old
       ones'. See Skocpol, Theda, 'Wallerstein's World Capitalist System: A
       Theoretical and Historical Critique', American Journal of Sociology,
       Vol. 82, No. 5, 1977, p. 1089.

the United States it would require several times the resources which we believe the world to possess. Perhaps the next global revolution would be the desperate fight for an equitable share of a shrinking cake. The energy crisis of those years, moreover, pointed to an accretion of wealth by elites in a few fortunate third world countries whilst the saddest effects were experienced by other third world countries with no petroleum. Such a view conjoured up new vistas for revolution within the inequitable oil rich countries, for conflict between third world nations and between what became known as north and south. Such discussions, however, proceeded outside the framework of the academic treatment of development. There the focus once again was on the internal functioning of nation states in the third world. The more optimistic thinkers argued that what had been fundamentally wrong with the dependency paradigm was its belief that third world countries had no control over their destinies. Indeed there was quite a range of choice to be found among modernising strategies if only ruling elites had the knowledge of their situation and the will to change it.

In the above scenerio the role of the social scientist was to be that of adviser. Revolutions, moreover, were not to be promoted by social scientists who neither knew how to make revolutions that ensured that the poor benefited nor had a right to sacrifice human life to their ignorance. This was the view of Michael Lipton who, writing in the latter half of the 1970s[89], identified the major problem facing third world states as a conflict between rural and urban classes. It was the rural sector which contained most of the poverty; yet it was there that one could find most of the low-cost sources of potential advance. In the urban sector, on the other hand, there was most of the articulateness, organisation and power. Excessive urban bias was not a result, as Pye believed, of the random and unsystematic adoption of western structures. Nor, as Frank believed, was it the result of the structure of global dependence. It was a consequence of the ethos inherited from the West by modernising elites.

The main argument was that peasants with little land, rather than constituting a drag on the process of development, were usually more efficient in their use of capital than huge capital-intensive industrial enterprises. Because of the urban ethos, however, the successful richer peasants tended to invest their profits in urban developments which had already attracted the bulk of government funding and which were favoured by industrial goods which were high priced in relation to agricultural produce. By the second half of the 1970s, Lipton estimated that less than 20 per cent of the investment available for development went into agriculture despite the fact that 80 per cent of the very poor (with incomes of less than one US dollar per week) depended on agriculture for their subsistence. Such a situation was irrational since the impact of one dollar of carefully selected investment in agriculture produced two to three times more benefit than investment elsewhere. The remedy was obvious! Governments should favour agriculture with cheap loans, fertiliser subsidies and the like, which would boost productivity, mop up unused labour and augment national wealth.

Yet most third world countries pursued contrary policies. The abuse of 'the green revolution' (which required expensive inputs and could favour

---

89. Lipton, M., Why Poor People Stay Poor: A Study of Urban Bias in World Development, Temple Smith, London, 1977.

the already rich), and the rising cost of petroleum (which affected the provision of tractors, farm machinery and fertilisers) served as pretexts for claiming that the cost of agricultural development was too high. In the meantime, a rural 'brain drain' had occurred where the bright youngsters from rural areas trained in the cities for urban jobs. In a situation where the best of very scarce resources were diverted to the cities, Lipton could only complain:

> Much cant is talked about the justice of violence to counter hidden state violence, and about the identity of poverty, exploitation and violence, but it is not cant to stigmatise as violence the diversion of health resources to kidney machines, whilst villagers suffer infant mortality rates as high as one in five for want of the simplest medical care.[90]

The diagnosis is indeed apt, but what of the remedy? It is only urged that social scientists explain the causes of poverty in the hope that third world governments will listen. The social scientist's capacity is after all 'to analyse; he has no special talent for administering governments or revolutions' (or even university departments).[91] Here, we have the converse of the dependency paradigm. That paradigm offered an analysis of the structure of power without any remedies for overcoming poverty. Lipton offers us an analysis of the causes of poverty without any remedy for changing the structure of power. Given a market integrated society with free labour mobility, who can prevent the educated youth moving to the cities or overseas in search of a highly paid job? Is the necessary cultural revolution possible without some coercive measures promoted by the state?

Modernisation and Revolution: The Case of China

Our observation that the relationship between the urban and rural sectors in third world countries is inextricably entwined with the structure of state power is clearly exemplified in the case of China. In the early 1950s that country pursued a developmental strategy, copied from the Soviet Union, which discriminated against the rural sector in favour of the rapid development of heavy industry. By the mid 1950s, it became clear that this strategy was producing an investment crisis. The rural sector was not generating funds sufficiently quickly to continue the programme of heavy industrialisation. At that time decisions were taken to shift more attention to agriculture. It was evident, however, that many of China's leaders were unwilling to slow down the pace of industrialisation to accommodate the new focus and a mammoth production drive was under-taken to 'advance' at high speed 'on all fronts'. The ensuing Great Leap Forward soon ground to a halt amid very adverse climatic conditions. At a time of severe economic privation in the early 1960s, the Chinese government stressed most strongly its committment to agricultural

---

90. ibid., p. 269

91. ibid., pp. 328-52.

54.

priority. Yet once again industrial development outstripped agricultural development.

It seemed, therefore, that a fundamental switch to agriculture was extraordinarily difficult to bring about. What were the reasons for this? First and most important was the belief amongst Chinese planners that rapid economic development required a very high rate of capital accumulation. This could best be achieved by paying low prices for agricultural goods whilst keeping industrial prices high. In 1956 Mao Zedong warned against this without much effect. The urban bias, it seems, was not just a consequence of inherited attitudes but was somehow inherent in the system. Of course, Mao Zedong was no Lipton. He had no intention of strengthening market relations in the countryside. On the contrary, he became the principle exponent of mass mobilisation to achieve production goals - a policy which in retrospect contributed even further to imbalance in favour of the urban areas.

It is fairly clear why Mao endorsed priority to agriculture but baulked at the fostering of rural market relations. These, it was felt, could contribute to the furtherence of capitalism. Such was what he felt to have happened in a subsequent period when Party control over the rural areas was more relaxed. By that time (the early 1960s), Mao was also concerned with a much bigger problem - the extent to which groups with much power and high status were abusing their position. In short he feared the growth of a new class which would stand in the same relation to the means of production as the old classes which the original revolution had overthrown. The result was to be the Cultural Revolution which began in 1966.

The Cultural Revolution took as one of its primary aims the overcoming of what Mao defined as 'three major differences' - between town and country, worker and peasant and mental and manual labour. It was premissed on a very new conception of revolution which held that continual struggle had to be directed against not only the vestiges of the past but embryonic exploiting groups which were continually thrown up in the course of economic development. Those groups were primarily urban groups. But the paradox of the Cultural Revolution was that the revolutionaries themselves were predominately urban. Throughout vast areas of the countryside, the Cultural Revolution left the peasants untouched. In the end the urban struggle was to have bad economic results, whilst the peasants seemed only willing to respond to what many of the cultural revolutionaries had seen as concessions to capitalism.

After 1978, it seems, the Chinese Communist Party switched to dealing with the gap between town and countryside by non-revolutionary means. The urban-rural terms of trade were changed radically in favour of the peasants. At first sight, this would seem to be a step towards eliminating the 'three major differences'. Such a view, we contend, is somewhat superficial. Clearly one of the results of the new policy is that peasants producing a significant surplus will be better off than before. Those near to the town who are able to sell part of their produce on the free market will experience considerable rises in income. But those rural units without a considerable surplus may be expected to lag behind the remainder and intra-rural inequalities will grow.

But still, it may be argued, the general gap between town and country is closing. But such is a rather economistic view. One must look at how the new policies are rationalised. In the past it could be argued that the gap between urban and rural areas was the consequence of the need for a high level of savings to lay the basis for a new society. In the meantime efforts to close the gap might be undertaken by transferring skilled personnel to the rural areas, by decentralising services and light industry and raising the level of education in rural schools. Now the gaps which remain are described in technological determinist terms, i.e. as the inevitable consequences of the level of development of the Chinese economy. They will change as modernity is diffused from centre to periphery. If such is the case why should peasants bother to stay in the countryside and do their best to build up the rural areas; why not migrate to the centre if one can persuade (or bribe) authorities to relax the controls on mobility?

And so we are back to a trickle-down view of development promoted by a leadership which is seen more and more to have a vested interest in continued inequality. Enough of the old revolutionary spirit remains for the Communist Party to attempt to stamp out graft and corruption. But how far is such graft and corruption seen as systemic? It is seen no longer as the product of the present but of the vestiges of feudalism. It is being countered by a leadership, which for all its concern about the urban-rural terms of trade, is still ineradicably urban and determined to stay so. Indeed that leadership no longer has to worry about being sent to the countryside during a political campaign.[92]

Here we are back to the argument of the last chapter. Konrad and Szelenyi as well as Gouldner, it will be remembered, argued that a new class might develop on the basis of policies pursued by an urban elite. That elite might win over the peasants by improving the urban-rural terms of trade but will it solve any more dimensions of the contradiction between worker and peasant, town and country and mental and manual labour? Suburban peasants are not so disadvantaged but the desire to go to the town and participate in the work of rational redistribution is so much greater. So indeed is the desire of many urban dwellers to go abroad to the source from which development trickles down.

One question stands out in stark simplicity. Is the sociologist Max Weber right and does modernisation inevitably lead to bureaucratisation?[93] Do all revolutions become routinised and is continuous revolution, as promoted by Mao, a utopian dream? Or are there different kinds of modernisation and different kinds of rationality? This is the point with which we began the preceding chapter.

Conclusion

Many of the diffusionist theorists used to argue that revolution was the result of strains caused by the early stages of Western induced modernisation and could be expected to disappear as modern societies came into existence. They were supported by a lot of social psychological literature which related 'relative deprivation' to the stages of economic growth. Since the heyday of diffusionism, however, the world has become much

92.   Hu Yaobang, 'Speech at the Meeting in Celebration of the 60th Anniversary of the Founding of the Communist Party of China', July, 1981, Chinese Communist Party, Resolution on CPC History, (1949-81). Foreign Languages Press, Beijing.

93.   See Rheinstein, Max, Max Weber on Law in Economy and Society, Harvard University Press, 1954.

more unstable, to the point where different kinds of relative deprivation look like continuing to recur throughout the forseeable future. The universal 'J curve' of the late 1970s and early 1980s has highlighted the fact that the world economic recession affects third world countries differently. Some prosper at the expense of others whilst some thirty or so countries seem doomed to perpetual poverty. In such a situation it is difficult to generalise about the prospects for diffusion.

The dependency theorists, we have argued, adopted a mirror image of the diffusionist view, seeing revolutions (in the narrow sense) as the product of temporary problems in the incorporation of peripheral regimes into the all-pervasive world capitalist order. Eventually, however, one could conceive of a new revolutionary age once the possibilities for expansion were exhausted. Vietnam was not, as many thought, the beginning of the end, but that end would surely come. Nevertheless, once it became clear that some parts of the periphery were experiencing significant economic growth and that the arguments about surplus were faulty, the paradigm was dropped. In retrospect, it is quite apparent why dependency theory was of little use in anticipating the occurrence of revolutions. It was inherently backward-looking. In a sense even more marked than is implied in diffusionist theory, history was an extrapolation from the present; this is nowhere more apparent than in Wallerstein's treatment of the old periphery east of the Elbe.

The reformist reaction against dependency theory explicitly refuses to consider revolution; it being beyond the competence of the social scientist. But if the next series of revolutions in the world is to be fought out for shares of a declining cake, some knowledge of the division of that cake would be of great value. Nowadays it is becoming increasingly clear that only the romantic economist (a strange creature in a 'dismal science') believes that resources may be created indefinitely. In a finite world there has to be global redistribution or a kind of global apartheid. In either case the result will almost certainly involve violent revolution. We noted in the last chapter that Marx saw the consequences of capitalist modernisation as either socialism or barbarism, while Max Weber saw the consequences of modernisation as entrenched bureaucracy. In the former scenario, if barbarism is to be avoided, the social scientist must not plead, as does Lipton, that he has no special knowledge of revolution. In the latter scenario, Lipton's view that first world social scientists will precipitate redistribution by offerring their analyses, would seem to be somewhat naive.

INDEX

INDEX

Huntington, S., 42-4

ideational and sensate cultures, 27, 32, 37
India, 7, 13, 17, 30, 42
Indo China, 39
    Kampuchea, 46
    Vietnam, 46, 49, 57
Indonesia, 29, 46, 48
involution, 28-9
intellectuals, 18-22, 33, 35-6
Iran, 28-9, 36, 39-41, 43
Islam, 4, 40-1
Italy, 5, 22
Ivan III, 19
Ivan IV, 13, 19-20

James II, 5
Japan, 13, 15-6, 33, 36, 40, 46
Johnson, C., 30, 33-4, 37, 39, 42, 46

Khrushchev, N., 32
Konrad, G., 17-22, 35, 37, 52, 56
Korea, 39, 41
Kropotkin, P., 25-6, 31
Kuhn, T., 2-3

Latin America, 45, 49-51
legitimation, 18-9, 21-2, 35-6
Lenin, V., 12, 20, 30, 39, 43
liberalism, 4-5, 7, 23-4, 26, 30, 33, 40, 50
Lipton, M., 53-5 57
Lukacs, G., 2

Mao Zedong, 29-30, 55-6
Marcuse, H., 34-7
market relations, 1, 5, 8, 13-21, 39, 51-2, 55
Marx, K., and Marxism, 1, 5, 7-12, 17-9, 23, 26, 28, 31-3, 37, 42-4, 48, 57
Maslow, A., 47
Mexico, 50

Mill, J.S., 24
Mind, universal (Zeitgeist), 1, 22-6, 28, 36
Montesquieu, C., 6, 23
Moore, B., 13-7, 19-20, 22, 36-7, 46
multilinear approaches, 1, 3, 7-22, 36
Mussolini, B., 22

Nagy, I., 29
Napoleon I, 24, 50
Napoleon III, 24
Nesvold, B., 46

objective idealism, 1-3, 22-31, 36

patrimonialism and prebendalism, 19-20, 22
peasant revolts and revolution, 9, 15-7, 30
Peru, 51
Peter I, 19-20
Pol Pot, 46
Poland, 22, 39
Polanyi, K., 18
political development, 6-7, 41-2
production, mode of, 2, 7-8, 10-13, 18, 31-3
    Asiatic, 10-13, 19-20
progress, 1, 7, 27, 29, 41-2, 48
Pye, L., 40-41, 53

rationality, 1, 21-3, 35, 40
relative deprivation, 45-8, 56-7
resources crisis, 52-3, 57
revolution,
    bourgeois, 3, 5, 10, 13-6, 18, 30, 36-7, 43-4
    cultural, 2-3, 5, 7, 19, 21, 25-32, 36, 39, 54-5
    disease model, 26-7
    industrial, 5, 36
    green, 53-4
    managerial, 3, 19, 24, 33, 37

INDEX

Puritan, 5, 7, 13-4, 40
Roman Empire, 4, 7-10, 20, 30
Romania, 11
Romein, J., 29
Roosevelt, F., 33
Rostow, W., 39, 44, 48
Russia, see Soviet Union

Sahlins, M., 29
Saint-Simon, H., 23-4, 31
'second serfdom', 15, 20, 51-2
Service, E., 29
Singapore, 38
slavery, 8-10, 14, 20
social psychology, 44-8, 56
sociology, 23-5
Sorokin, P., 26-8, 31-2, 37, 46
South East Asia, 40
Soviet Union, 6-7, 12-3, 15-7, 19-
22, 26, 28-9, 32-4, 38, 43, 45,
51, 54
Bolshevik Revolution, 6, 12,
21, 26, 28-9, 45
Spain, 22, 27, 50
Spencer, H., 25
Stalin, J., 2, 12, 32, 36
structural functionalism, 33-4, 39-
42, 49
Sweden, 17
Switzerland, 17
Szelenyi, I., 17-22, 35, 37, 52, 56

Taiwan, 38-9
technological determinism, 1-3,
24-5, 31-6, 39-41
telos, 18-9, 21-2, 28, 31-2
Tocqueville, A. de, 44, 47
Trotsky, L., and Trotskyism, 30,
32

U Ne Win, 51
United States, 1, 6-7, 13-4, 17,
22-3, 33, 37-8, 43-5, 48-9, 53
Civil War, 13-4

Revolution (18th century) 14,
22-3, 44
urbanisation;   see cities and
countryside

Velasco, J., 51
Vietnam; see Indo China
violence, 26, 28-34, 37, 42, 46-8,
54

Wallerstein, I., 51-2, 57
Weber, M., 3, 5-6, 56-7
Wertheim, W., 3, 28-31, 35-7, 41-
2, 45-8
Wittfogel, K., 12-3, 19-21
'world system', 9, 38, 49-52, 57

Yaroshenko, L., 32
Yugoslavia, 6